Disclaimer

The information in this guide is for general purposes only. While we've made every effort to ensure it's accurate and helpful, the author cannot guarantee its completeness or reliability. Use this guide at your own risk.

Hiking and outdoor activities involve risks. By using this guide, you accept full responsibility for your safety and well-being while exploring. Always check local rules, trail conditions, and weather updates before starting your hike.

The author is not responsible for any injuries, losses, or damages that may result from using this guide or participating in activities mentioned here.

Contents

Chapter One: Welcome to Eastern Europe.

1.1 Why Hungary, Romania, and Bulgaria?

Some trips go slowly. Not in terms of time lost, but in how your comprehension grows with each step. Something starts to alter as you go from the cobblestone alleys of Budapest to the foggy woods of Transylvania, and finally down to the sun-drenched coasts of Bulgaria's Black Sea. You stop comparing and start absorbing. You start being present.

Hungary, Romania, and Bulgaria do not vie for attention in the same manner that other Western European nations do. They do not need to. Instead, they gradually show their true beauty, which is lived-in, worn, and covered with memories. It's the type of beauty that hasn't been cultivated for tourists—it's been formed by generations of people who continue to meet for weekly market days, decorate eggs by hand at Easter, and pass down recipes that haven't changed in 200 years.

This portion of Europe is a crossroads. Traces of the empire may be seen everywhere: Ottoman mosques, Austro-Hungarian façade, Roman ruins, and Soviet-era residential complexes all share the same sky. However, none of these nations are just relics of the past. In truth, the true satisfaction comes from how alive they are—how strongly they uphold history while accepting change in their own, sometimes modest, manner.

Hungary entices you with grandeur and rhythm. Budapest has that picture image, with Parliament soaring above the Danube, bridges illuminated at night, and steamy thermal springs nestled amid baroque and art nouveau structures. But go outside the capital and you'll find wine-soaked valleys, fairytale towns, and traditions like folk dance that are still practiced in village halls. The meal is robust, the friendliness is genuine, and the pace is slower than you'd anticipate.

Romania provides excellent contrast. Cities like Bucharest are rough and bold, with vibrant street art and a burgeoning artistic scene. However, only a few hours away, time seems to stand still in towns like Maramureș, where people still harvest hay by hand and wear traditional attire on Sundays—not for display, but because it is who they are. You'll encounter painted monasteries that resemble open-air art galleries, woods resounding with birdsong, and ancient villages that feel like they're from a fairy tale—if fairy stories had Wi-Fi and delicious coffee.

Bulgaria may surprise you the most. It is kind, giving, and proud of its mountains, music, and memories. Plovdiv hums with activity, and its Roman theater continues to stage plays beneath the sky. Sofia has a combination of old and modern spirit, with golden-domed cathedrals meeting Soviet monuments and small cafés serving lavender lemonade beside communist bookshops. Head south to see monasteries nestled between peaks, while the coast provides sun-drenched beaches, old villages, and a zest for life that makes every meal feel like a festival.

These nations have a profound human dimension. They haven't been formed to suit tourists; instead, they encourage you to meet them for who they are. You will not have to dress up your experience. Instead, it will come to you in moments: a granny selling handmade cheese at a roadside stand, a folk band performing in the town center, or a stranger insisting you sample a taste of their homemade plum brandy. It's not about chasing the highlights; it's about focusing on what's genuine.

If you're coming here for the first time, you don't have to know everything. You only need to come interested, open, and prepared to go at the region's own pace. In exchange, these nations will provide you with something that will stay long beyond your return journey home: tales worth sharing, meals worth remembering, and the quiet satisfaction that comes from finding a place that most tourists never get the opportunity to fully experience.

1.2 How to Use This Guide.

Whether you're preparing months in advance or reading through pages on the train between towns, this book will help you travel with greater confidence, depth, and knowledge.

It's designed for a wide range of tourists, from solitary explorers to couples, budget-conscious friends, and families looking for new experiences. You don't have to be an experienced traveler or cultural enthusiast. What counts is your curiosity and desire to try something new.

Here is how this guide works best:

Start with the basics - Chapter 2

Before getting into places, look into vacation planning tools. You'll get candid advice on when to go, what to take, how to smoothly pass borders, and how to avoid the stress of visa complications or missing trains. Everything is stated straightforwardly and plainly, particularly if you are new to this location.

You'll also discover sections on cultural etiquette and linguistic suggestions to assist you in not only avoiding mistakes but also engaging with locals in meaningful ways.

Country by Country - Chapters 3, 4, and 5.

Hungary, Romania, and Bulgaria each have their specialized chapters, organized by city and area. Every location includes clear, practical advice on where to stay, what to eat, how to get about, and which attractions are worth your time and money. Beyond the iconic sites, we emphasize smaller, more soulful experiences, such as family-run vineyards, tucked-away hiking paths, and tiny cafés that offer handmade jam with their tea.

We also include area insights, seasonal information, and advice on whether to visit early (or late) to avoid crowds. And we don't shy away from the truth—like when a castle isn't worth the admission cost or when a walk is more difficult than it seems online.

Connect the Dots, Chapter 6

If you're putting out a cross-border itinerary, this chapter lays it all out: where to begin, how much time to allow yourself, what mode of transportation works best, and what type of pace to anticipate. Whether you have 10 days or three weeks, you'll discover intelligent, adaptable itineraries focused on culture, nature, or hidden gem experiences.

Go Deeper - Chapters 7 and 8.

This is when we draw back the curtain. These chapters look at how history, religion, and folklore influence daily living, from ancient Thracian graves to Orthodox pilgrimage routes to mountain stories that linger in people's minds. We also take you into the wild: hiking trails, national parks, natural springs, and other outdoor experiences that will fully rejuvenate you.

Stay Practical, Chapter 9

This is your toolset. Safety recommendations, SIM card hacks, health resources, money-saving methods, public transportation alternatives, and advice on how to dress stylishly (and politely) in every season. It's straightforward, simple to use, and intended to let you travel with confidence.

For the Heart - Chapter Ten

We conclude with a chapter on the spirit of travel: the books, films, music, and crafts that may strengthen your connection to these places. Consider it a preparation for your trip—or a means to carry it with you long after you've returned.

Bonus Tools - Chapters 11 and 12.

You'll discover maps, language cheat sheets, city transportation guides, and local transit hubs to help you get about easily. The last chapter includes a heartfelt thank you, insights from the author, and room for your notes and tales.

This tutorial is not just about logistics. It is about traveling with mindfulness. About meeting people where they are, appreciating culture without romanticizing it, and allowing for unexpected discoveries. You'll certainly receive practical information, but you'll also get genuine, unpolished, people-first travel advice that will help you get the most out of every day on the road. So, no matter where you are on your journey—dreaming, planning, or already in motion—this book is for you. Let's dig in. Let us begin.

Chapter 2: Plan Your Journey

2.1 Best Time to Visit: Seasons and Festivals

The annual rhythm varies somewhat over this area. Farmers in the villages continue to monitor the skies for the first signs of frost. Festivals set the rhythm of cities, from spring flower fairs to harvest wine festivities to cinnamon and pine-scented Christmas markets. The ideal time to visit Hungary, Romania, and Bulgaria is dependent on your desired experience.

You are not only selecting the weather. You're selecting the mood, speed, and cultural texture.

Spring (April to early June): Quiet Beauty and Clean Air Spring arrives slowly but with purpose. Lilacs blossom in Sofia's streets, while daffodils bloom along the pathways around Lake Balaton. The air smells fresh, crisp, and lively. Crowds are sparse, costs are more reasonable, and residents are pleased to see activity returning to parks, cafés, and marketplaces.

Thermal spas in Hungary remain hot even under chilly skies. Transylvania in Romania begins to green up, as the woodlands around Brașov fill with songbirds. Bulgaria's hiking trails are at their most tranquil, and rural guest houses have opened for the season. Sofia's Jazz Festival and Hungary's Spring Festival start the season with music, cuisine, and outdoor entertainment.

What to wear: Bring a warm layer and a lightweight waterproof jacket. Spring days are lovely, but nighttime temperatures drop drastically.

Summer (mid-June to August): Lively, hot, and open late.

If you like lengthy days and vibrant evenings, this is it. Lake beaches are humming, beer gardens are filled, and cultural festivities are in full flow. Lake Balaton in Hungary serves as the country's unofficial summer capital, with families swimming, couples sailing, and villages like Tihany offering lavender fields and open-air performances.

Romania's castles are most gorgeous, but also the most busy, so early mornings are your best bet. The hay making season in Maramureș is in full swing, and the rural settlements are at their most alive. Meanwhile, Bulgaria's Black Sea coast is

fully awake: from Nessebar's peaceful appeal to Sunny Beach's party scene, there's something for everyone.

Keep in mind that summer brings heat, particularly in places like Bucharest and Sofia, where temperatures often reach 35°C (95°F). But it is also festival season. From Budapest's Sziget Festival to Romania's Electric Castle and Bulgaria's Rozhen Folklore Festival, this is when the area comes alive.

What to wear: Dress in cool, breathable layers. Pack a swimsuit, sunscreen, and comfortable walking footwear. A lightweight scarf or hat is useful for sun and temple visits.

Autumn (September–mid-November): Golden Light, Fewer Tourists

Autumn may be the most underappreciated season to visit. The heat has mellowed. Across the Carpathians, trees burn yellow and rust. Vineyards in Hungary and Romania are bustling with harvest activities. The foggy mornings in Transylvania add to Bran Castle's gothic beauty, while the mountain paths in Bulgaria are crisp and ideal for trekking.

Wine festivals begin in destinations such as Tokaj and Dealu Mare. In Sofia, art fairs and independent film festivals begin to fill the chilly nights. Prices begin to fall, and there is more space to breathe, both in museums and on buses.

What to wear: Layers again—the weather in fall changes quickly. Warm sweaters, a raincoat, and comfy boots are your go-to.

Winter (late November–March): Cozy Traditions & Magical Snow

If you like unhurried travel, winter will reward you in subtle ways. Fairy lights glitter around the cities. Budapest's Christmas markets, located beneath the Parliament Dome, include spiced wine and kürtőskalács (chimney cake). In Romania, rural life becomes more personal and authentic—wood smoke in the air, horses hauling sleighs, and Christmas carolers singing by candlelight.

Bulgarian ski resorts such as Bansko and Borovets provide good value for snow fans. In areas like Sinaia, you may ski and tour castles on the same day.

Travel is slower at this time of year—expect occasional delays—but if you're prepared for snow, you'll enjoy an old-world winter without the crowds.

What to pack: Bring thermal layers, a thick coat, waterproof boots, and gloves. Public locations are well-heated, while rural travel needs appropriate attire.

2.2 Entry Requirements and Visas

This area may seem strongly linked, but it is not yet a fully integrated EU experience, particularly at border crossings. Here's what you should know to minimize delays at passport checks and travel freely between nations.

Visa Overview: What is the Schengen Zone and who belongs to it?

- **Hungary and Bulgaria** are both Schengen countries (as of March 2024).
- **Romania** entered the Schengen Zone for air and sea travel only, so if you're flying in from another Schengen nation, you won't have to go through another passport check. However, land crossings (such as trains and buses from Hungary) may still need an ID check.

If you are a traveler from the EU, UK, USA, Canada, Australia, or New Zealand, you will normally be permitted 90 days visa-free for 180 days in the Schengen Zone. Simply verify that your passport is valid for at least 3-6 months after your entrance date and has at least one blank page.

Crossing Borders by Land: Plan Your Route

Bus and rail travel between these nations is fairly common. Due to Romania's limited Schengen membership, border inspections at land crossings are to be expected. Officers may board trains to verify passports, particularly at night.

Pro tip: Prepare your paperwork before the stop. This includes not just your passport, but also any evidence of lodging or departure ticket, particularly if you are going one-way.

Other essentials:

- Children under the age of 18 may need supplementary paperwork while traveling without both parents.

- Some nations need a visa; check with each country's embassy well in advance of your travel.
- Travel insurance is not required for all tourists but is strongly recommended.

Insider Tip: Entry stamps are important. If you want to travel in and out of Schengen nations, keep track of your days. Overstaying might result in significant penalties or restrictions.

2.3 Transportation and Border Travel.

This area is simple to navigate—if you know a few tactics. The distances may seem to be tiny on a map, but geography, train quality, and national infrastructure disparities may all contribute to longer journey times. So, instead of focusing just on distance, consider context and connection.

By Train: Scenic, Affordable, but Sometimes Slow
Trains are romantic and frequently gorgeous, particularly in Transylvania and over Bulgaria's highlands. However, they are not always the quickest solution.

- **Hungary** provides the most dependable and quick service. Trains between Budapest and Debrecen or Pécs are regular and pleasant.

- **Romania's** trains may be attractive yet sluggish, particularly on mountainous lines. Delays are usual, so bring food and be flexible.
- **Bulgaria's** network is developing, with clean and low-cost intercity services. Sofia to Plovdiv is a popular short hop.

When crossing borders, **use international trains or combine tickets. For example,** the trip from Budapest to Bucharest is direct (although it will take more than 14 hours). Consider breaking it into stops like Debrecen or Cluj.

Booking Tips:

- Use national rail websites or applications. In Hungary, MÁV; Romania, CFR; and Bulgaria, BDZ.
- Night trains are available, although in limited numbers. Book early for sleepers.
- First class is not always required, although it is affordable and often worth the added luxury.

Bus: Quick, Cheap, and Border-Savvy

Long-distance buses (FlixBus, EuroLines, etc.) link most major cities and may easily traverse borders. They are frequently quicker than railroads between capitals, although less picturesque.

- Direct bus travel from Budapest to Sofia takes around 8 hours.
- The journey from Bucharest to Sofia takes around 6-7 hours, including a brief rest break at the border.
- Luggage is generally supplied, but check beforehand.

Local tip: If traveling by bus from Romania to Bulgaria, bring cash for restroom breaks since many border rest places do not take cards.

By Car: Freedom and Flexibility (with Caveats)

Renting a vehicle provides unparalleled access to countryside treasures—fortresses, rural monasteries, and distant villages—but you must be okay with small roads and sometimes confused signs.

Border crossings by automobile are simple, however, you will need:

1. Green card insurance (certain it covers all three countries).
2. Vignettes (road toll stickers) for highways in Hungary, Romania, and Bulgaria are available online and at petrol stations near borders.

Parking in city centers may be a hassle. In rural places, there is little tension.

In Summary:

- Trains: ideal for scenic routes; slower yet soothing.
- Buses are dependable, inexpensive, and efficient for traveling between cities.
- Car rental is good for flexibility and is handy outside of cities.
- Borders are straightforward but still active—keep paperwork accessible and anticipate quick stops, particularly when entering or departing Romania.

2.4 Budget and Travel Costs

First and foremost, going through Hungary, Romania, and Bulgaria is quite beneficial. You're not compromising quality; you're just accessing a region of Europe where your money still goes farther, your meals are home-cooked, and kindness is often free of charge.

However, prices might vary based on your travel style, season, and whether you're drinking wine on a family vineyard or ordering drinks at a hip rooftop bar in Bucharest.

Here's how to budget wisely, spend strategically, and yet feel well rewarded.

Currency Cheat Sheet.

- Hungary utilizes the Hungarian Forint (HUF).

Approximately 1 EUR = 390-410 HUF (rates vary often).

Coins are only in forints; minor transactions, like metro tickets or street food, may still need cash.

Romania uses the Romanian Leu (RON).

Approximately 1 EUR equals 5 RON.

Prices are often cheaper than in Western Europe, particularly in rural regions.

Bulgaria uses the Bulgarian Lev (BGN).

Pegged to the Euro, 1 EUR = 1.95 BGN.

Credit cards are becoming more widely used in cities due to their stability and ease of conversion.

Pro Tip: While some hotels, taxis, and cafés in tourist districts may take euros, always bring local cash, particularly for public transportation, street food, and country goods.

Daily Budget Estimates

The following are realistic daily ranges per person, excluding flights:

Budget Style	Hungary (€)	Romania (€)	Bulgaria (€)
Shoestring (Hostels + Markets)	30–45	25–40	25–35
Mid-Range (Guesthouses + Restaurants)	60–90	50 80	45–75
Comfort/Flashpacker (Hotels + Wine Tastings)	100–140	80–120	70–110

Accommodation:

1. Hostels cost €10-20 per night (higher in larger cities).
2. Boutique hotels or guesthouses cost €35-60 per night.
3. Upscale hotels cost €70-150 per night (sometimes including breakfast and spa access in Hungary or ski resorts in Bulgaria).

Food:

1. Street food or bakeries cost €1-3.
2. Local lunch meals cost €5-8.
3. Dinner with wine costs €12-25.
4. High-end eating costs €35-50 (still affordable by Western standards).

Transport:

1. The cost of a journey on the city metro or tram is between €0.50 and €1.50.
2. Intercity train: €5–25, depending on distance.
3. Car rental is €25-40/day plus petrol.
4. Buses are reliable and affordable (Sofia to Bucharest costs about €15).

Attractions:

1. Museums and castles cost between €2 and €10. Student discounts are frequent.
2. Guided excursions or activities cost €10-30.
3. Spas and thermal baths cost €10-20 (half or full-day entry).

Saving Smart Without Missing Out

- **Eat locally:** Daily menus (typically 2-3 dishes) are a traveler's best-kept secret, particularly in Romania and Bulgaria.
- **Use city cards:** Budapest, Plovdiv, and Bucharest all have multi-day tickets that include museum admission and transportation.
- **Travel slowly:** The area favors slow travel. You will save money on transportation and get more expertise.
- **Walk or ride the local tram:** Many historic towns are compact. Walking or jumping on old streetcars (such as Budapest's Tram 2) adds character at no expense.

Cash, Cards, and ATMs

- Visa and Mastercard are widely accepted, particularly in cities.
- Always carry a little amount of cash, particularly in smaller towns, and rural locations, and for tipping.
- ATMs are secure and frequently accessible, but to avoid hidden costs, pick ones affiliated with banks rather than freestanding currency kiosks.
- Avoid dynamic currency conversion and always choose to be charged in the local currency.

Tipping Culture

- In Hungary, restaurants often charge 10%; round up minor amounts.
- Romania: 10-15% at restaurants; €1-2 for porters and drivers.
- Bulgaria: Similar—a 10% gratuity is welcomed. In taxis, round up to the closest level.

Money in this context is more than simply a mathematical concept; it is also about relationships. That €4 glass of local wine is more than simply a deal; it represents a narrative, a region, and a family vineyard. So budget sensibly, spend thoughtfully, and don't be afraid to tip lavishly when someone goes above and beyond—as they often do.

2.5 Language and Cultural Etiquette.

You don't have to know the language to connect here, but making an honest effort to acquire a few words can go a long way. The area prizes kindness, friendliness, and respect for customs—even the clumsiest "hello" in the native tongue may result in smiles, discounts, and, on occasion, an additional helping of dessert.

Languages at a glance.

- **Hungary**: Hungarian (magyar)

A distinct and sophisticated language unconnected to most others in Europe. English is commonly spoken in Budapest and the surrounding tourist towns.

- **Romania is Romanian.**

Consider it a Latin-based Romance language, similar to Italian or French. English is widely spoken among young people.

Bulgaria: Bulgarian.

- A Slavic language with Cyrillic writing. In cities, signage often contains the Latin alphabet. In villages, gestures may be your best option.

Simple phrases that may go a long way.

English	Hungarian	Romanian	Bulgarian
Hello	Szia / Helló	Bună ziua	Zdravey
Thank you	Köszönöm	Mulțumesc	Blagodarya
Please	Kérem	Vă rog	Molya
Cheers!	Egészségedre	Noroc!	Nazdrave!
Yes / No	Igen / Nem	Da / Nu	Da / Ne

Practice Tip: *Learn these five words and speak them with a smile; people will immediately soften. Bonus points for writing them phonetically in your notes.*

Cultural Norms and Social Etiquette

- **Greetings:** A strong handshake and eye contact are common in all three nations, particularly among males. When you arrive in rural Romania or Bulgaria, you may be welcomed with a kiss on the cheek or a shot of plum brandy.

- **Respect the senior generation:** Whether on a tram or at a rural market, give your seat and talk nicely to elders; it is really appreciated.

- **Churches and monasteries require** modest dress, with shoulders and knees covered. Women may be requested to wear a headscarf at certain Orthodox places.

- **Shoes off:** Many local households, particularly in Bulgaria and rural Romania, require you to remove your shoes upon entry. Slippers are often given.

- **Don't haggle too much:** Bargaining is more popular at marketplaces than in stores or restaurants. Do it with a grin and gentleness; this is a game, not a conflict.

- **Toasting is religious,** particularly in Romania and Bulgaria. If someone offers you a drink, take at least a sip; declining outright may be deemed disrespectful. Look your buddies in the eyes and toast "Noroc!"" alternatively, "Nazdrave!""

A Final Word on Hospitality.

Someone you just met may offer you handmade jam, local brandy, or even lodging for the night. Hospitality is firmly ingrained in all three cultures, particularly in rural regions. Accept with grace, provide modest presents if living with locals (chocolate, postcards from your native country), and always express gratitude.

Traveling here is more than simply viewing sites. It's about being accepted into someone's world, even if just for a time. A little language, curiosity, and friendliness may go a long way.

Chapter 3: Hungary – Tradition & Thermal Waters

3.1 Budapest highlights

Evenings in Budapest appear to evolve into something more than merely dusk. The city does not become silent; rather, it starts to sparkle. Lights wave off the Danube, trams glide past art nouveau buildings, and laughing emanates from a ruined tavern hung with colorful lamps in the courtyard of a collapsing pre-war structure. It isn't only scenic. It feels alive beneath your skin.

Hungary's capital is commonly referred to as the "Pearl of the Danube," but it doesn't completely describe it. Budapest is more than simply gorgeous; it is multilayered. Elegant but rough. Traditional and forward-looking. It strikes a balance with history while being unapologetic. A city where centuries-old hot spas are only streets away from ruin bars, where you can spend the morning bathing in mineral pools under frescoed ceilings and the evening dancing to Balkan rhythms with locals and expatriates alike.

This is a city to remain in, not simply travel through. And it rewards those who delve just under the surface.

The Essentials

- **Buda and Pest:** The Danube separates the city into two different sections. Buda is the calmer, hillier, more residential side, with castles, thermal springs, and panoramic views. Pest is flatter and busier, with cafés, pubs, markets, and nightlife.
- **The currency is the Hungarian Forint (HUF).** The card is commonly accepted, however carries cash for markets and smaller restaurants.
- **Getting Around:** Budapest features one of Europe's most efficient metro, tram, and bus networks. The M1 metro (continental Europe's oldest!) is a delightful method to travel between monuments. Tram 2 goes along the river, offering picture vistas.

Top Experiences in Budapest.

1. Soak Like a Local: Thermal Baths

Thermal bathing is not a luxury; it is a way of life. Begin with the famed Széchenyi Baths, which have outdoor pools surrounded by Neo-Baroque buildings. Arrive early or late for less crowds. The Gellért Baths provide a more tranquil experience, with stunning art nouveau décor and mosaic pools.

Insider tip: Bring flip-flops, a towel, and a swim hat (lap pools demand one). Most bathrooms offer lockers and rent towels for a charge.

When to go: Early in the morning for a peaceful atmosphere. Evening trips, particularly in the winter, are wonderful, with steam rising into the freezing air.

2. Ruin Pubs and the Seventh District

Once-abandoned buildings in the Jewish Quarter have been transformed into ruined pubs—bohemian, artistic, mismatched havens of music and creativity. Begin in Szimpla Kert, the original ruin bar, where each room seems like a separate world—bathtubs for sofas, chandeliers constructed from bike parts, DJs nestled amongst antique TVs and plants.

What to order: Try a local spritzer or Tokaji wine. Food offerings often include goulash, street burgers, and vegetable bowls.

3. Castle Hill with Fisherman's Bastion

The panoramic views from Fisherman's Bastion are stunning, particularly around dawn or blue hour. Wander the cobblestone lanes, stop at Matthias Church with its brilliant tiled roof, and go inside Buda Castle, which houses the National Gallery and History Museum.

4. The Danube promenade

One of the most enjoyable walks in the city. Start from the Parliament and go south along the river. Stop by the Shoes on the Danube Memorial—silent and profoundly emotional. Take a nighttime Danube river cruise for a beautiful view of the Parliament and lit bridges.

5. Parliament, Markets, and Street Food

The Hungarian Parliament Building is as majestic inside as it is outside; reserve a tour in advance. Then visit the Great Market Hall for paprika, pickles, chimney cakes, and leather products. Upstairs, sample lángos (fried dough topped with sour cream and cheese) and local sausages.

Quick Tip:

1. During peak season, make prior reservations for baths and Parliament tours.
2. Tipping: Leave around 10% at restaurants unless already included.
3. Stay central (Districts V, VI, or VII) for easy access to major attractions and nightlife.

3.2 Exploring Beyond Budapest

Hungary is more than just its capital. Trains and buses make it simple to travel, and within a few hours, you may visit wine regions, lakeside resorts, old fortifications, and Mediterranean-style villages steeped in Roman and Ottoman history.

3.2.1 Eger

Eger, nestled in the Bükk Mountains of northeastern Hungary, is a laid-back community. Locals stroll between pastel-colored houses and lush squares, and everything seems to be infused with the aroma of wine and slow-burning wood.

Eger is well renowned for its baroque architecture and red wine, particularly the full-bodied Egri Bikavér ("Bull's Blood"), which can be tasted in centuries-old wine cellars cut into volcanic rock in the Valley of the Beautiful Women (Szépasszony-völgy).

But there is more than just wine. Climb to Eger Castle, where Hungarian warriors previously fought off Ottoman invaders. Visit the Minaret, a thin 40-meter-high tower left over from 17th-century Turkish domination, and climb it if you dare. Explore Eger Basilica and the Archbishop's Palace, or take a trip to the thermal baths for a relaxing dip surrounded by woods.

Travel Tips:
1. Eger is about 2 hours by rail from Budapest.
2. Many vineyards provide complimentary sampling when you purchase a bottle.
3. Walk or bike to the valley; taxis charge tourist rates.

3.2 Lake Balaton

Hungarians call Balaton the "Hungarian Sea"—and for good reason. Stretching over 77 km, this is Central Europe's largest freshwater lake, and a beloved summer playground.

Balaton offers something for every traveler:

- Balatonfüred is elegant and charming, with lakefront promenades, stately homes, and spa hotels. An excellent platform for wine tastings.
- Tihany Peninsula: A highlight, with lavender fields, Tihany Abbey, and hiking routes that provide lake views.
- Siófok is a popular spot for parties. If you're seeking nightlife, live music, and beach clubs, this is the place.
- Keszthely is known for its royal Festetics Palace and relaxed atmosphere, with easy access to thermal Lake Hévíz.

You may ride around the lake (special cycling paths are available), sail, paddleboard, or just swim and relax beneath the chestnut trees. Each coast has a distinct flavor: the north is wine country and hills, while the south is flat and beachy.

Travel Tips:
- Trains from Budapest take around 2 hours to Balatonfüred or Siófok.
- Summer weekends are packed; go midweek or in May/early September for more room.
- If you prefer electronic music by the sea, look out for the Balaton Sound Festival in July.

3.2.3 Pécs

Pécs, located in southern Hungary near the Croatian border, combines Mediterranean appeal with cosmopolitan heritage. It's cozy, creative, and quietly amazing.

Stroll down Király Street, where cafés spill onto the sidewalks and live music fills the air in the evening. Admire the Pécs Cathedral, which has green towers and frescoed interiors. Visit the Early Christian Necropolis, a UNESCO World Heritage site, to see Roman graves and mosaics concealed under contemporary streets.

What makes Pécs so unique is its Ottoman legacy—the city was dominated by Turks for 150 years, and their influence can still be seen in the Mosque of Pasha Qasim, which is today utilized as a Catholic church.

Art aficionados should take notice that Pécs is home to Hungary's famed ceramic artist, Zsolnay, whose glittering eosin glaze tiles adorn buildings around the city. The Zsolnay Cultural Quarter is a creative hotspot with galleries, workshops, and museums distributed around a campus-like environment.

Travel Tips:
1. Pécs is about 2.5 hours from Budapest by rail.
2. Try the native white wines from neighboring Villány, which are crisp, mineral-rich, and very underestimated.
3. Don't miss the sunset from Tettye Park, which offers panoramic views of the town below.

3.3 Hungarian Cuisine.

The fragrance frequently reaches you before the plate—smoky paprika, rich meat cooking gently, and sweet yeast pastries crisping in the open air. Hungarian food is robust, generous, and rooted in rich, earthy comfort. It is a cuisine molded by history—Ottoman, Austrian, and Slavic—as well as geography, with rich plains and river valleys feeding kitchens that honor seasons and traditions.

You do not only eat in Hungary. You eat a lot, even if it's just lunch.

Staple Dishes to Know and Love

Gulyás (goulash)

Not a thick stew, but a rich, paprika-laced soup that is meaty and comforting. Traditionally prepared in a cauldron over an open fire, it combines meat, potatoes, carrots, and peppers to create something considerably more than the sum of its components. Gulyás may be found on practically every restaurant menu, but for the whole experience, try it in a rural csárda (tavern).

Lángos

This golden deep-fried flatbread is Hungary's unofficial food. The basic form is covered with sour cream and grated cheese, although sweeter versions (such as garlic butter or Nutella) are also popular. Best served fresh from a market stand, particularly in Budapest's Central Market Hall.

Paprikás csirke (chicken paprikash)

Tender chicken cooked in a creamy paprika sauce with nokedli (mini egg dumplings). A comfort food staple that serves as an easy introduction to paprika-heavy cooking.

Hortobágyi Palacsinta

A savory crêpe loaded with ground pork and topped with paprika sauce and sour cream is more than just a pancake; it's almost like a meal wrapped in memories.

Halászlé (Fisherman's Soup)

Spicy, brilliant red, and cooked with river fish (typically carp), this dish is particularly popular near the Danube and in southern Hungary. It's an acquired taste, but locals swear by its winter-warming properties.

Sweets that speak to your soul.

Dobos Torte.

A show-stopping cake with five to seven thin layers of sponge, chocolate buttercream, and a crackling caramel topping. József Dobos created it in the 1880s to survive longer without refrigeration, and it quickly became a national favorite. Best savored in Budapest's renowned Gerbeaud Café.

Kürtőskalács (Chimney Cake).

Originally from Transylvania, now popular across Hungary. The dough is rolled, coiled around a wooden spit, roasted over the fire, and then coated with cinnamon sugar or nuts. What was the result? Crisp on the exterior, pillowy within, and extremely delicious.

Rétes (Hungarian Strudel).

Thinner than Austrian counterparts and often stuffed with sour cherries, poppy seeds, or sweetened cottage cheese. Look for them at village bakeries and rural markets, where the fillings vary seasonally.

Flavors of Hungary: Spices, Wines, and Markets.

Paprika is more than simply a spice; it represents an identity. From sweet to spicy, smoked to ground, it distinguishes Hungarian cuisine. It's everywhere: braided strands in marketplaces, red tins at souvenir shops, and liberally blended into practically every savory food.

And then there's wine. Hungary's vineyards may not get as much international attention, but that only offers more **potential for exploration. Try:**

1. Tokaji Aszú, sometimes known as the "wine of kings," is a golden dessert wine with a honeyed flavor and deep complexity.
2. Egri Bikavér, from Eger, is strong, pungent, and profoundly crimson.
3. Olaszrizling and Furmint are crisp, white wines perfect for summer drinking.

Visit Budapest's Great Market Hall, or a small market outside the city, to enjoy local cheese, honey, cured meats, and homemade pickles.

Dining Tips for First-timers

1. **Meal Times:** Lunch is the main meal of the day; many restaurants provide a "menu of the day" (menü) at a wonderful price.
2. **Tipping:** 10%-12% is typical unless already included.
3. **Dietary Requirements:** Vegetarian choices are expanding, although traditional diets rely heavily on meat and dairy. Look for menus with the words "reform Konya" (modern kitchen) or "vegetáriánus" in cities.
4. **Don't think twice about street food**. Street cuisine in this city is both fresh and satisfying, whether it's lángos, strudel, or hot sausages from a vendor.

3.4 Festivals, Folk Art, and Traditions.

Hungary's traditions are not relics, but live threads woven throughout everyday life. You'll see it in the needlework on a grandmother's shirt, the beat of a folk dancer's boots, and the pleasure with which a teenage guy plays his violin during a harvest festival.

These aren't contrived performances; they're sincere sentiments handed down through families, lovingly renewed by younger generations, and cherished equally in tiny towns and on major stages.

Folk Traditions and Handicrafts

- Matyó embroidery, originating from the hamlet of Mezőkövesd, has colorful flower motifs in red, yellow, and blue. Frequently spotted on blouses, aprons, and table linens. It is more than simply ornamental; it has cultural significance, with motifs representing protection, fertility, and local identity.
- Kalasz and Kalocsa Designs: Similar to Matyó, but more pastel or white-on-white, and often employed in exquisite lacework or painted ceramics.
- Easter eggs (Hímestojás) are intricately colored and scratched, with patterns varying by area. During Húsvét (Easter), males traditionally spray ladies with perfume (or cold water!) as a fertility ritual turned into spring amusement.
- Hollókő, a UNESCO World Heritage site, is a living museum of Hungarian rural life, including wood carving and pottery. Visit during a festival to observe artists at work, traditional clothing worn proudly, and streets filled with music.

Hungarian Festivals to Experience

Busójárás (Mohács, February).

A chaotic and spectacular carnival in which men dressed in wool cloaks and carved devil masks use fire, noise, and joy to drive away winter. It's profoundly symbolic and exciting, with roots in pagan rites and Ottoman resistance.

Budapest Spring Festival (March / April)

A two-week festival of art, theater, and music in Budapest. There will be classical music as well as experimental dancing.

Debrecen Flower Carnival (August 20).

Debrecen bursts in color on Hungary's national festival, with gigantic flower floats, folk parades, and fireworks.

Hollókő's Easter Festival

Step back in time. Traditional garb, egg painting, folk singing, and plenty of water play in a hillside community that seems to have stood the test of time.

Wine Harvest Celebrations (September–October)

Harvest season in Tokaj, Villány, and Eger consists of grape stomping, open cellars, music, and feasts. Locals and guests mix during tastings and bonfires.

Music and Dance

- **Csárdás** is a classic Hungarian folk dance featuring slow, dramatic introductions that transition into fast-paced twirls and stomps. It's more than simply performing; it's narrative.
- **Táncház Movement:** "Dance houses" where traditional music and dance are taught and maintained; particularly popular among young Hungarians who want to revive folk culture. Ask around in Budapest or Szentendre for events that are available to guests.
- **Folk Instruments:** The cimbalom (a sort of hammered dulcimer) and tarogató (a woodwind with a sorrowful voice) are essential to Hungarian folk music. Hear them perform live at festivals or local folk bars.

Tips for Connecting with Tradition.

1. To learn more about regional distinctions, visit an ethnographic institution such as the Hungarian Heritage House or Budapest's Institution of Ethnography.

2. Purchase locally produced items directly from artists, particularly in smaller towns or at festival stands.
3. If you are asked to a community festival, say yes. Even if you do not speak Hungarian, your presence is appreciated.

Hungary does not retain tradition in glass exhibits. It is alive—in dancing, in stitches, and in the tales told over pálinka by the fire. Step into it with open arms and a little curiosity, and you'll leave with something much more valuable than trinkets.

Chapter 4: Romania's Castles, Carpathians, and Count Dracula

4.1 Bucharest: Old Meets New.

It does not take long to see that Bucharest defies simple categorization. One minute you're walking through an elegant arched gateway from the nineteenth century, and the next you're passing a concrete block engraved with street art, its balconies blossoming with artificial gardens. The streets hum—not only with automobiles and trams, but also with contrast, endurance, and a perpetual confrontation between the past and future.

Locals drink espresso in century-old cafés with cracked marble tables or get craft beer from a pop-up bar nestled inside a disused printing press. This is not a city stuck in the past; it is always moving, building, and questioning, with one eye on its narrative and the other on what comes next.

Explore Bucharest Like a Local

Lipscani District (Old Town).

Lipscani was formerly the city's commerce core, and it is now a mix of cobblestones and contrasts. Today, when you walk through its small streets, you'll see centuries-old inns, busy nightlife venues, antique booksellers, and trendy boutiques. Step into Caru' cu Bere, a renowned beer hall with stained-glass windows and hearty Romanian cuisine. Don't just come; stay, sit outside, and watch the parade of life pass by.

Palace of Parliament

This is the world's heaviest building, commissioned by tyrant Nicolae Ceauşescu. The space is massive, with 360,000 m² of marble, chandeliers, and football-field-sized carpets. Take the guided tour for a direct glimpse at Communist ambition and the contradictions of extravagance in an era of national adversity.

Romanian Athenaeum and Revolution Square

The center of Romania's cultural and political renaissance. Attend a performance in the Athenaeum—acoustically and visually stunning—or stand on the plaza where the 1989 revolution erupted, overthrowing decades of dictatorships. It's more than simply history; it's live memory.

Carousel's curriculum

Possibly one of the most stunning bookshops in the world. Housed in a renovated 19th-century structure, its white spiral stairs and floating balconies encourage you to spend hours browsing Romanian literature alongside English versions. Head upstairs for tea and breathtaking views of the Old Town roofs.

Bucharest Travel Tips

- Transport: The subway is quick and convenient; taxis are inexpensive but need a meter. Ride-sharing applications (such as Bolt) are commonly utilized.
- Language: English is widely spoken among younger natives, particularly in the hotel industry. Learning a few Romanian words always brings happiness.
- Bucharest is typically secure, however, be cautious around popular nightlife areas. Keep a close watch on your stuff, particularly at Old Town bars.
- Stay in Lipscani for the atmosphere or Cotroceni for leafy serenity and easy access to museums and parks.

4.2 Transylvanian Treasures

Stepping beyond the city, Romania resembles a fairy tale, with fortified cathedrals, Saxon villages, and towns that seem to have been painted from memory. Transylvania is more than myths and misty hills; it's a genuine, breathing place where medieval meets contemporary, and every hill appears to have a tale.

4.2.1 Braşov

Braşov is an ideal starting point for exploring Transylvania. Nestled at the foot of the Carpathians, it is a city surrounded by woodlands, fortified by fortifications, and filled with quaint squares and Saxon history. The streets swirl softly past pastel facades and Gothic arches, each encouraging you to calm down.

Begin at Piaţa Sfatului (Council Square), the medieval center, where street musicians perform under 15th-century towers and people enjoy coffee in the fresh mountain air. Then go to the Black Church, which called after surviving a massive fire and today houses one of Europe's biggest pipe organs. If you attend a concert here, the acoustics are cathedral-level amazing.

Take the cable car or trek to Mount Tampa for spectacular views and picnic opportunities. And in the evenings? Brașov's pub and bistro scene is modest and charming, with local wines, Transylvanian comfort cuisine, and cozy lighted nocks.

Brasov Travel Tips

1. Stay inside the ancient city walls for charm and walkability.
2. Don't miss Rope Street (one of Europe's narrowest), historic military bastions and turrets, and the adjacent ski resort of Poiană Brașov.
3. Eat locally: Try sarmale (cabbage rolls), ciorbă de burtă (sour tripe soup, which is more excellent than it sounds), or papayas.

4.2.2 Sibiu and Sighișoara.

Sibiu has the sense of a city suited for strolls and snatched afternoons. Its buildings have eyes, literally. The baroque roofs have thin attic vents that resemble drowsy eyelids, lending the city a watchful, fairytale appeal. It was formerly the capital of the Saxon area and is now an attractive combination of German precision and Romanian flair.

Begin at Piata Mare (Big Square) and go to the Bridge of Lies (which, according to mythology, creaks when someone lies). Explore Romania's oldest museum, the Brukenthal Palace, and take a trip up to the Evangelical Cathedral to watch the sunset over the city's red rooftops.

Meanwhile, Sighișoara is a UNESCO World Heritage Site that resembles a medieval stronghold. Colorful residences line the summit. Clock towers chime. Tiny churches emerge from corners, and at dark, lamps flash along cobbled paths formerly frequented by Saxon merchants—and, reportedly, Vlad Țepeș (Dracula), who was born here.

Sibiu and Sighişoara Travel Tips

1. Base yourself in Sibiu for comfort and culture, then take a day excursion to Sighişoara (or stay overnight for candlelight calm).

2. Sibu's Theater and Jazz Festivals attract large audiences, so book your lodgings early.

3. Look for artists offering hand-painted pottery, woven carpets, and wooden toys in both towns.

4.2.3 Bran Castle.

Bran Castle is positioned on a cliff, just spectacular enough to pique centuries of imagination. And, although it's often referred to as "Dracula's Castle," the reality is more complex. Although Vlad the Impaler never resided here, generations of people have drawn parallels between fiction and myth.

That being said, Bran Castle is well worth a visit—not for the vampire myth, but for how it depicts decades of Romanian history, from royal families to peasant insurrection. The chambers twist and swirl in surprising ways, with tight stairs, medieval weaponry, and antique furnishings from Queen Marie's day.

Wander the gardens, climb the towers, and then visit the local market right outside, where sellers offer anything from sheepskin jackets and Dracula mugs to handcrafted preserves and cheeses wrapped in bark.

Bran Castle Tips

- To avoid bus tours, arrive early (before opening) or late (1-2 hours before closure).
- Wear strong shoes; the steps inside are steep and uneven.
- For an exciting addition, combine with the neighboring Râșnov Fortress or go on a woodland trek surrounding Zărnești Gorge.

4.3 Maramureș & Bucovina

In northern Romania, time slows to a heartbeat as wood smoke rises from chimneys, poultry nibble along the roadside, and church bells beckon not just to prayer but also to continuity. In Maramureș, centuries-old rituals are not only for visitors; they are part of daily life.

Here, wooden churches tower like sentinels, some with delicate spires that seem to grasp for heaven. Many are UNESCO-listed, carved without nails, decorated with fading paintings inside, and shingled like fish scales outside.

Look for Bârsana, Poienile Izei, and Ieud—each hamlet offering a glimpse into folk orthodoxy and communal spirit. On Sundays, locals continue to dress traditionally—not for display, but because it has always been done that way. If you're fortunate enough to be welcomed inside a house, you'll be served handmade cheese, plum brandy (țuică), and a seat by the stove as if you were family.

In adjacent Bucovina, the atmosphere lightens, the hills widen, and the famed Painted Monasteries dazzle with paintings that wrap around the exteriors like comic books. Sucevița, Voroneț, and Humor Monastery are treasures of religion and folklore, each depicting saints, wars, and blessings in vibrant blue, red, and green.

Travel Tips for Northern Romania.

- Maramureș is best accessible by automobile, however, there are trains to Sighetu Marmatiei and buses to the villages. Consider hiring a local guide to tour the hidden hamlets.
- If possible, visit on a Sunday to observe complete traditional attire, music, and church services.
- Suceava serves as the regional center în Bucovina, offering vehicle rentals and monastery visits.

4.4 Outdoor Activities in the Carpathians

Up here, where the air is pine-crisp and the solitude is broken only by birdsong or the crunch of your footfall, Romania seems untamed in the nicest sense. The Carpathians are more than simply a background to stories; they are a playground for adventure. Whether you're trekking through floral meadows, horseback riding through glacial valleys, or crossing rustic rope bridges into bear territory, this is Romania at its most raw and authentic.

The Carpathians form a broad arc over the nation, hiding a vast wilderness of forests, alpine meadows, and remote communities where time moves at a different pace. The trails here are more than simply routes; they weave a living symphony of mythology, nature, and struggle.

Hiking & Trekking: Where to Start

Piatra Craiului National Park

Dramatic limestone hills, tiny pathways that cling to cliffs, and postcard-worthy vistas. Hike the Zărneşti Gorge, a deep, mossy canyon reminiscent of a Tolkien scenario, or take a ridge trek to Cabana Curmătura and spend the night in a mountain hut.

- 🥾 Ideal for intermediate to experienced hikers.
- 🔔 Getting There: Zărneşti is readily accessible by rail or automobile from Braşov.
- ⛺ Insider Tip: Bring snacks and water; huts provide basic meals, but availability varies.

Făgăraş Mountains and Transfăgărăşan Road.

This mountain range, known as the "Alps of Transylvania," is Romania's tallest and wildest. The Transfăgărăşan Road, made famous by Top Gear, winds between these summits, offering breathtaking bends and vistas. From there, walk to Bâlea Lake or attempt Moldoveanu Peak (2,544 m), the country's highest.

- 🚗 Access: The road is open from late June to October, but may be blocked by snow during other seasons.
- ■ Keep in mind that weather may change quickly, so pack layers and check predictions before leaving.

Retezat National Park

One of the most pristine areas in the Carpathians. Glacial lakes reflect the sky like mirrors, and the vegetation here is old and unique. There won't be many people—just wild goats, profound solitude, and the sound of the wind over the heights.

- Stay in nearby towns like Hațeg or Cârnic.
- 🐻 Be Bear Aware: Bears are part of the ecology, therefore make noise on paths and avoid hiking alone after dark.

Other outdoor pursuits

Wildlife Watching

Romania has the greatest number of brown bears in Europe. While seeing one in the wild is unlikely (and better left to chance), you may participate in an ethical bear hide experiment conducted by conservationists who value animal care in sites like Zărnești or Tusnad.

Horseback Riding

Riding is still an integral part of rural Transylvania culture. Stables în Sighișoara, Măgura, and Viscri provide guided excursions through meadows, villages, and woodland paths. Beginners are welcome; the horses here are robust and friendly.

Caving and Via Ferrata

Explore a karst environment dotted with caverns in the Apuseni Mountains, including Scărişoara Ice Cave, which holds Europe's biggest subterranean glacier. Meanwhile, the Carpathians provide via ferrata (iron trail) climbing routes protected with ropes and ladders, ideal for adrenaline seekers.

Skiing and snowboarding

Poiană Braşov, Sinaia, and Predeal are the most popular ski resorts in Romania during the winter. They're cheaper than Alpine resorts, making them great for families or novices, with lots of après-ski mulled wine and substantial cuisine.

Adventure Essentials and Responsible Travel Tips.

- 🥾 Dress appropriately and in layers since the weather in the mountains may quickly change.
- Use apps like Maps.me or Romania Hiking Map (offline) for accurate trail guidance.
- 🧭 If hiking alone, let someone know your path. In distant regions, cell signals may diminish.
- ⚫ Pack everything. Rural routes may not have bins; respect the wild.
- 🐻 Avoid feeding animals and trek with care in bear zones (clap or talk quietly to signal presence).

- ● ◗ By supporting small guides, local lodges, and family-run eco-hostels, you can help maintain communities.

The Carpathians are not conquered. They enter with respect, patience, and a desire to slow down. It's not a race to the peak. It's about traveling through nature in a manner that makes you feel tiny and happy to be here.

4.5 Romanian Food and Drinks.

Romanian food has a generous spirit. Whether you're in a hamlet kitchen or a metropolitan restaurant, each meal seems as if it was prepared for a visitor who had just arrived from the cold. It's unpretentious comfort cuisine that is truly regional and influenced by Ottoman, Hungarian, Saxon, and Balkan traditions, all cooked together in pots seasoned with tales.

The cuisine is hearty, the amounts are generous, and if you leave hungry, it is your own.

Enjoy these staples.

Sarmale (cabbage rolls)

Ground pig (or mixed meat), rice, and herbs are wrapped in sour cabbage leaves, slow-cooked in tomato broth, and often served with mămăligă (creamy polenta) and sour cream. Served during festivals, funerals, weddings, and Sunday luncheons.

Mici (grilled sausages)

Short, skinless sausages made with minced meat (pork, lamb, or beef), seasoned with garlic and spices, then cooked until juicy and browned. Best eaten on the street with mustard and toast, ideally in the sunlight.

Ciorbă de Burtă (Tripe Soup).

An acidic, creamy soup prepared with beef tripe, vinegar, garlic, and sour cream. It's more popular than you'd think, with a cult following. If you're hesitant, try ciorbă de pui (chicken) or vegetarian options with root vegetables and lovage.

Tochitură

A substantial stew with pig pieces cooked in tomato sauce, topped with mămăligă, cheese, and fried egg. It Is popular in Moldavia and mountainous areas.

Hearty Breads and Sides

Mămăligă

Cornmeal prepared like polenta is a simple, pleasant dish that can be found on almost every Romanian table. Serve with stews, cheeses, grilled meats, or just butter and sour cream.

Zacuscă

A smoky vegetable spread prepared with roasted eggplant, red pepper, and onion, frequently produced in the fall and eaten on crusty bread. Jars may be found at marketplaces or given as gifts by hosts "just because."

Beef Salate

A celebratory meal similar to Russian salad, consisting of chopped cooked vegetables and meat (or fish) joined with mayo and arranged like a celebration cake.

Sweet Finishes

Papanasi

A deep-fried sweet cheese doughnut topped with sour cream and fruit preserves. One of Romania's most renowned sweets, it's virtually hard to just have one.

Cozonac

A celebratory sweet bread filled with walnuts, poppy seeds, or chocolate. Common around Christmas, Easter, and family gatherings.

Drinks with depth.

Śuică & Palincă

Strong plum or fruit brandies are offered in small glasses before meals. Frequently handmade and strongly regional. Drink slowly—this isn't vodka; it's legacy in a glass.

Romanian Wine

Romania is a secret treasure for oenophiles, with over 6,000 years of winemaking history. Try:

- Fetească Neagră (red): Dark, peppery, and delicious with grilled meat.
- Grasă de Cotnari (white) is aromatic and semi-sweet.
- Tămâioasă Română: Muscat-like, flowery, and delicious with cheese.

Local beers

Ciuc, Ursus, and Silva are national favorites. Microbreweries are rapidly growing, particularly in Cluj and Bucharest.

Dining Etiquette and Tips.

- 🔔 Enjoy your meals without rushing.
- 🍴 Most traditional restaurants automatically serve bread and pickles.
- 💬 Compliment your host or server and inquire about their recipes—they will be proud.

- In restaurants, a tip of 10% is considered courteous and appreciated.
- 🍴 If invited to a local's home, bring a modest gift, such as wine, candy, or flowers.

Food in Romania is more than simply a source of nutrition; it also represents hospitality, identity, and continuity. Whether you're eating grandmother's soup or sampling wine in Moldova, you're being welcomed into a way of life.

Chapter 5: Bulgaria - Mountains, Monasteries, and the Black Sea

5.1 Sofia: Capital of Contrasts

Mornings in Sofia follow a pattern that is both familiar and unexpected. Locals drink cappuccino on sidewalk chairs under Art Nouveau balconies, while only a few yards away, an old man sells handmade socks next to the remains of an ancient Roman street. Sofia, a city at a crossroads between East and West, Orthodox and Ottoman, Soviet and spiritual, does not aim to impress; rather, it urges you to delve deeper.

You may begin your day inside the Alexander Nevsky Cathedral, one of the world's biggest Orthodox cathedrals, filled with candlelight and chanting. But you might just as easily start at a street market where grandmothers sell herbs by the fistful and smoked cheese wrapped in linen. Sofia doesn't tell just one tale; it tells many at once, which is what makes it so compelling.

Must-see sights in Sofia
Alexander Nevsky Cathedral

This church, with its dazzling golden domes and large interior packed with icons and flickering lighting, serves as Sofia's spiritual heart. It was built to remember Russian troops who died during the liberation from Ottoman domination and is a site of peaceful majesty. Step inside with respect—men often remove their hats, and even visitors remain silent.

Ancient Serdica Ruins with St. George's Rotunda

The bones of Roman Sofia lay under the slick glass of the Serdika metro station, including streets, residences, and bathhouses going back almost 2,000 years. Just beyond is the St. George Rotunda, a red-brick church from the fourth century that is still in use today. Mass here seems like walking back in time.

The Largo and Socialist Era Sofia

A short stroll will take you to Sofia's impressive Stalinist architecture, which includes the old Party House. Keep an eye out for mosaics, Soviet sculptures, and massive public squares—memorials of a past that is both despised and remembered with ambivalence. The contrast between this and the surrounding Roman remains is striking.

Vitosha Boulevard and Local Life

Sofia has a pedestrian heart. Lined with stores, ice cream carts, cafés, and designer boutiques, it's the ideal area to people-watch or grab a refreshing drink with locals in the evening. Finish your journey with a visit to South Park, a lush oasis for picnickers, rollerbladers, and walking couples.

Food and Culture Tips in Sofia

1. Drink ayran (a salty yogurt drink) at any corner kiosk; it's both refreshing and local.
2. Visit a local bakery early to get banitsa (cheese-filled pastry) when it is still fresh from the oven.
3. Join a free walking tour—they're daily, interesting, and take you through layers of history.
4. Visit Vitosha Mountain: Easily accessible by bus or cab, this wooded mountain provides panoramic views, hiking routes, and even skiing in the winter.

Sofia is not flamboyant. It's textured, friendly, and surprisingly layered—a location that encourages leisurely exploration, pleasant discussion, and a desire to delve into the gaps between.

5.2 Plovdiv, Europe's Timeless City.

Plovdiv is one of those cities in which the past and current coexist together. A youngster skateboards on Roman paving stones, as a violinist performs under the arches of a 2,000-year-old theater. It's a city where you may turn a corner and be transported to another century, followed by another.

Plovdiv, often regarded as Europe's oldest continuously inhabited city, is more than just a history lesson; it's a warm, lively, lived-in environment where every structure seems to have a background.

Explore Plovdiv's Old Town and Beyond
Ancient Roman Theatre

This amphitheater, which is still used for summer performances, is cut into the hillside and has remarkable acoustics as well as magnificent views of the city. If you can catch a live performance here—opera, jazz, or Shakespeare—it's sheer enchantment beneath the sky.

Old Town Plovdiv

Wander slowly. The streets are steep and uneven, but they are lined with brilliant 19th-century Revival villas painted in vibrant ochres, blues, and rust reds, complete with

Ottoman-style overhangs. Visit the Ethnographic Museum, which is housed in a lovely merchant house and teaches about Bulgarian rural life and crafts.

Kapana (The Trap)

Plovdiv's creative neighborhood, formerly crowded with workshops, is now home to independent galleries, coffee roasters, bookshops, and murals. Grab a craft drink, start up a conversation with a local, or peruse design boutiques offering handcrafted ceramics and embroidered T-shirts.

Nebet Tepe Hill

This is one of Plovdiv's seven hills, and it contains ancient Thracian remains and provides a panoramic view of the city. It is particularly attractive after sunset when couples and visitors peacefully watch the roofs sparkle.

First-Time Tips in Plovdiv.

1. Base yourself in Kapana for easy access to everything and a friendly neighborhood atmosphere.
2. Climb slowly—Old Town is steep, with cobblestones that need proper footwear.
3. Eat like a local: In the summer, try kavarma (slow-cooked pork stew), grilled veggies with sirene cheese, or tarator (cold cucumber yogurt soup).
4. Although many people know English, a simple smile and a few words like blagodarya (thank you) may go a long way.

In Plovdiv, history is not hidden behind glass; you can walk through it. And yet, it never seems like a burden. It seems like a lovely, live discussion that you're invited to join.

5.3 Mountains and Monasteries

As you travel into the highlands, the city hum disappears, leaving behind the stillness of pine, the sound of cowbells in a faraway meadow, and the echo of chants wafting down chilly stone halls. Spirituality and environment are inextricably linked in Bulgaria, and this is most evident in the country's mountains and monastic sites.

Rila Monastery, Bulgaria's Spiritual Heart

The Rila Monastery, located high in the Rila Mountains, is more than simply a religious landmark; it is also a national emblem. Founded in the 10th century by St. Ivan of Rila, it has survived fires, invasions, and centuries of history. Nonetheless, it remains firm, its striped arches and colorful paintings evoking dedication, craftsmanship, and pride.

Stepping into the inner courtyard, you'll be surrounded by cascading balconies, black-robed monks, and a calm devotional mood. Inside the cathedral, the paintings are a kaleidoscope of saints and biblical themes, with every inch covered in color and significance.

- 🛏 Tip: Stay overnight at the monastery guesthouse for basic rooms, early morning bells, and a chance to enjoy the calm before the throng.
- 🥾 Take a short hike to St. Ivan's cave, a hermitage where the saint once dwelt.

Rhodope Mountains: Where Earth Meets Legend

These calm, pine-draped mountains in southern Bulgaria are rich in mythology, music, and medicinal plants. The Rhodopes, said to be Orpheus' home, offer an ethereal quiet and a rich legacy of mythology, bagpipe music, and storytelling.

Highlights:

1. Shiroka Laka is a hamlet known for its stone buildings, piper festivals, and some of Bulgaria's most evocative folk music.
2. Yagodina Cave and Devil's Throat Cave are vast subterranean networks full of stalactites and stories. The Devil's Throat is believed to be the gateway to the underworld.
3. Trigrad Gorge: Sheer cliffs rise spectacularly above twisting mountain roads, ideal for picture stops and wayside honey vendors.

Bachkovo Monastery — Art, Peace, and Pilgrimage

Bachkovo Monastery, located 30 minutes from Plovdiv, is smaller than Rila but as lovely. The courtyard is filled with grapevines, stone arches, and the faint murmur of travelers. Don't miss the ossuary up the hill, a modest church with 12th-century murals that are private and very emotional.

Plan Your Monastic Escape

- When entering active churches, dress modestly, with shoulders covered and no shorts.
- Be respectful: Remember that these are holy areas, even if you're simply appreciating the artwork.
- Combine monasteries with hiking: Many are located in or near national parks and woodland routes.

In Bulgaria's mountains and monasteries, you're not simply touring; you're slowing down, bonding, and experiencing something deeper. It's where tales are inscribed in stone, and calm comes not from solitude, but from a powerful feeling of place that makes you soften within.

5.4 The Black Sea Coast.

On Bulgaria's Black Sea coast, the pace slows. Mornings begin with soft sand under your toes, days go gently with seafood by the port, and evenings shine with a laid-back appeal as musicians tune their strings beneath beach sunsets. This isn't the glitz of the French Riviera or the hustle of Spain; it's softer, more grounded. The Black Sea combines history, emotion, and summer delight in one salty, sun-drenched sweep. Whether you're looking for ancient ruins on the beach, calm cobblestone alleyways fragrant with fig trees, or exuberant summer festivals when residents and tourists dance till daybreak, this coastline greets you like an old friend.

5.4.1 Varna—The Seaside Capital

Varna, nicknamed the "Marine Capital" of Bulgaria, combines beach life, Roman heritage, and young vitality. It's both a vacation town and a functioning port, with lush boulevards, stately 19th-century architecture, and a vibrant cultural life that lies underneath its laid-back facade.

Things To Do In Varna

Sea Garden (Morska Gradina)

This huge park stretches down the shore like a green ribbon. Families come for picnics, couples wander under tree canopies, and musicians fill the air with folk music and laughter. Don't miss the sunset vista at the dolphinarium—it's pure enchantment as the sky fades into the sea.

Roman Thermae Ruins

The Balkans' biggest Roman baths are located right in the middle of town. Towering arches and high stone walls suggest that this was once a thriving leisure center in the second century. Walk amid the ruins, feeling the weight of time.

Varna Archaeological Museum

Home to the world's oldest processed gold, which dates back to 4600 BCE. That is not a mistake; this treasure predates the Egyptian pyramids. The museum is a tranquil haven for history buffs.

Beach Life and Boardwalk

The center beach is easily accessible from the Sea Garden and has several beach bars (called "kapani") serving drinks, grilled seafood, and local beer. Just over the bridge, Asparuhovo Beach offers a more relaxed atmosphere.

Insider Travel Tips For Varna

1. ♨ July and August are prime months—book early and anticipate many crowds.
2. 🚗 Taxis are affordable, but negotiate a deal or use the meter.
3. Try midi na tiavata (mussels in a clay pot) or afraid (fried horse mackerel).
4. 🎭 Attend summer concerts at the Roman Theater or festivals in the Sea Garden.

Varna is more than simply a place to unwind; it's a place to breathe in the summer, wander through thousands of years of history, and appreciate the basic pleasures of life: sunlight, music, sea air, and a table full of shared cuisine.

5.4.2 Sozopol and Nessebar: Ancient Cities by the Sea

Sozopol and Nessebar, two of Bulgaria's oldest and most picturesque cities, sit on the Black Sea coast, kissing centuries of history. These aren't contemporary resort towns. They're open-air museums, full of calm poetry, stone-carved tales, and centuries-old balconies leaning into sea breezes.

Sozopol: Bohemian Spirit and Ancient Soul

Sozopol, founded by the Greeks as Apollonia in the seventh century BCE, has always attracted painters, poets, and visionaries. Today, it retains that atmosphere with open-air art galleries, little amphitheaters, and a picturesque waterfront ideal for a long stroll after nightfall.

Wander through the Old Town, where wooden buildings cling to the cliffs and stone churches rest in flower-filled courtyards. Explore the Archaeological Museum to witness Thracian and Byzantine treasures, or take a sunset boat from the marina.

- Visit in early September for the Apollonia Arts Festival, which combines theater, music, and art by the sea.
- 🍷 Enjoy a clifftop dinner with midi s oriz (mussels with rice) and a glass of cool Mavrud.

Nessebar - UNESCO Wonder of the Water

Nessebar, located on a rocky peninsula, is a UNESCO World Heritage site with over forty churches representing every important period of Bulgarian history. The town is tiny and walkable in a day, but don't hurry. Its meandering alleyways, little bakeries, and classic wooden cottages will entice you to stay longer.

Make sure to visit:

1. The Church of Christ Pantocrator combines Gothic and Byzantine elements to create a beautiful red and green stone exterior.
2. Ethnographic Museum - A look at coastal life and crafts.
3. Local bakeries - Where old ladies knead the dough before daybreak, and the aroma of warm bread pervades the streets.

Tips for visiting Sozopol and Nessebar.

- ■ Old Towns provide charm, while New Towns feature sophisticated hotels and nightlife.
- ■ Remember to bring a hat and drink since the summer heat may be intense on the stone streets.
- ■ Shop for handmade pottery, sea salt soaps, and lace from local craftsmen.

Sozopol and Nessebar are the kind of places that creep under your skin—quietly, without fanfare, and linger with you long after you leave. They remind you that the finest travel experiences frequently result from just being someplace lovely and allowing it to hold you for a time.

5.5 Flavors of Bulgaria

Bulgarian food is large, earthy, and passionately handcrafted. Every dish seems to have a grandmother's touch, and every table—whether in a metropolitan apartment or a mountain village—feels like an invitation to slow down, take another taste, and linger a little longer.

Banitsa

A flaky, spiraling pastry filled with sirene cheese and eggs is cooked till golden. Found in every bakery, every morning, and equally great hot or cold. Locals often pair it with ayran (a salty yogurt drink) or boza (a fermented wheat beverage with a moderate taste).

Shopska Salad

The Bulgarian flag on a platter, with sliced tomatoes, cucumbers, onions, roasted peppers, and a snowy mountain of grated sirene cheese. Add sunflower oil and a shot of rakia for lunch.

Kebapche

Grilled minced beef skewers seasoned with cumin and garlic, often served with fries and grated cheese. Street food excellence.

Lyutenitsa

A thick, smokey spread prepared with roasted red peppers, tomatoes, garlic, and eggplant. Served with bread or meat, or just spooned straight from the jar. Each family has their interpretation.

Meats, Mains, and Mountain Food

Kapama

A substantial stew of pig, chicken, sausage, rice, and sauerkraut cooked in a clay pot for many hours. Common in Bansko and the Pirin area.

Kavarma

Slow-cooked pork or chicken with onions, mushrooms, and spices, often served sizzling in a clay dish.

Patatnik

A grated potato pie from the Rhodopes, seasoned with mint and baked over low heat until crispy on the surface and soft within.

Tarator

A chilly summer soup made with yogurt, cucumber, garlic, dill, and walnuts. Fresh, light, and ideal for hot seaside days.

Desserts and Delights

Rose Petal Jam And Lokum

This jam, made from the famed Kazanlak roses, is fragrant and delicate. It may be spooned over yogurt, pancakes, or just savored with a glass of water. Lokum (Turkish pleasure) comes in three flavors: rose, walnut, and citrus.

Baklava, Tikvenik (pumpkin pastry)

Sweet, sticky layers of filo, honey, and nuts—or packed with spiced pumpkin for a distinct Bulgarian flavor.

Drink Up: The Bulgarian Way

Rakia

The national spirit. Made with grapes, plums, or apricots and served in miniature glasses with salad or meze. Homemade variants may be powerful; drink cautiously and always toast ("Nazdrave!").

Wine

The ancient Thracians were winemakers, and Bulgaria retains that practice. Try:

- Mavrud (red) - Bold and peppery, cultivated near Plovdiv.
- Melnik is earthy and silky, being from the southwest.
- Dimyat (white) - Crisp and flowery, perfect for beach nights.

Bulgarian yogurt (kilo make)

It is so iconic that it has its bacterium strain (Lactobacillus bulgaricus). Tart and creamy, it may be eaten with honey, fruit, or by itself.

Tips For Eating In Bulgaria

1. 💰 Enjoy multi-course dinners at extremely inexpensive prices.
2. 🧂 Traditional foods have more salt and oil; balance with salad and yogurt.
3. 🍷 Ask locals about mehana (taverns) for music, fire-grilled foods, and barrel-aged wines.
4. 🍵 Never decline a host's offer—eating together fosters trust and friendliness.

Food is more than simply nutrition in Bulgaria; it is also a symbol of hospitality, tradition, and culture. Sit down, pull off a piece of warm bread, clink glasses, and join the beat of a table that spans decades.

Chapter 6: Cross-Border Adventures

[Traveling across Hungary, Romania, and Bulgaria: Seamlessly and Soulfully]

Some travels focus on depth, while others are about discovery. However, now and again, a path connects the two, allowing you to transcend borders not just physically, but also culturally, gastronomically, and emotionally. That is the beauty of this place. In a couple of days, you may travel across three countries, hear three languages, and eat three completely different meals while feeling as if you've been through one rich, interrelated tale.

For first-time visitors, think of this chapter as a practical plan and inspiration guide. Whether you're looking for old-world charm, wine tastings, woodland monasteries, or rural drives where sheep have the right of way, you'll find it here—and it's ready for exploration.

6.1 10-Day Capital Route

Hungary, Romania, and Bulgaria's capitals are more than simply metropolitan centers; they're living museums filled with history. This tour is ideal for visitors with limited time who wish to explore the breadth of Eastern European history, culture, and everyday life. It's fast-paced yet extremely engaging if treated correctly.

🚩 Recommended Itinerary (10 days)

Day 1-3: Budapest (Hungary).

- Begin with hot baths: Szechenyi and Gellért are good for getting into the groove.
- At sunset, stroll around Castle Hill and cross the Chain Bridge for an unforgettable view of the skyline.
- Eat and drink like a native with goulash, chimney cake, and Tokaji wine.
- Don't miss District VII's ruin bars—they're quirky, moody, and unique.

Day 4-6: Bucharest (Romania).

- Take a straight overnight train or a short flight from Budapest.
- Walk along Victory Avenue to see castles, gardens, and surprising Art Deco jewels.
- Visit the Palace of Parliament—it's big, contentious, and breathtaking.

- If you want to experience Carpathian air or touch with Dracula legend, take a day excursion to Sinaia or Bran castle.

Day 7-10: Sofia (Bulgaria).
- Arrive by rail or overnight bus from Bucharest; inexpensive flights are also available.
- Explore Alexander Nevsky Cathedral, Roman ruins, and the bustling pedestrian street Vitosha Boulevard.
- Set aside a half-day to explore Boyana Church and the surrounding Vitosha Mountain paths.
- Grilled kebapche, Shopska salad, and live folk music await you in a traditional mehana (tavern).

🍷 Insider tips

1. **Trains vs**. Buses: Romania and Bulgaria have slower train networks, while long-distance buses (FlixBus, local operators) are often quicker and more dependable.
2. **Currency Alert:** Hungary utilizes the forint, Romania the leu, and Bulgaria the leva. Always carry some cash.

3. **Language Help:** Although English is frequently spoken among young people, learning greetings always brings a grin.
4. **Stay Connected**: Regional eSIMs, such as Airalo or Orange vacation passes, function well in all three countries.
5. **Border crossings**: Within the EU but not Schengen, passport inspections still occur; have your papers available.

This itinerary provides an excellent introduction to the region's cultural capitals—urban, grand, and contemporary, but steeped in millennia of history. You'll leave with a full camera roll, a brain full of history, and a strong desire to return.

6.2 2-Week Culture, Wine, and Nature Loop.

If you like variety—vineyards and towns, castles and cliffside monasteries, outdoor markets, and woodland hikes—then this two-week schedule is ideal. It's designed for people who choose depth over speed, and the encounters seem like secret handshakes from the place itself.

🏴 Recommended itinerary (14 days)

Days 1-3: Eger and Tokaj (Hungary).

- Begin at Eger, a Baroque treasure renowned for its castle and wine cellars cut from volcanic rock.
- Drink Egri Bikavér (Bull's Blood red wine) at the Valley of the Beautiful Women.
- Then, visit Tokaj, a UNESCO-listed wine area, to experience the world-famous sweet Tokaji Aszú.

Days 4-6: Maramureş (Romania).

- Travel into northern Romania via rail or vehicle.
- Stay at a guesthouse and wake up to church bells, fresh milk, and wood-fired bread.
- Visit wooden churches, and the Merry Cemetery, and take the steam-powered Mocăniţa train.
- This is rural Romania at its most real.

Day 7-9: Transylvania (Romania)

- Head south via Cluj-Napoca, Sighişoara, or Braşov, all of which have medieval beauty.
- Hike across the Apuseni Mountains, discover salt mines, or stay in restored Saxon homes.
- Don't miss Rupea Fortress or Viscri, a UNESCO village supported by Prince Charles personally.

Days 10–12: Melnik and Bansko (Bulgaria)

- Cross into Bulgaria across the Rila Mountains.
- Melnik, Bulgaria's wine capital, is a little village surrounded by sandstone pyramids and villas from the 18th century.
- Overnight in Bansko, the entrance to Pirin National Park and home to robust mountain cuisine.

Days 13–14: Plovdiv or the Rhodope Mountains

- End at Plovdiv, where you may celebrate your voyage with craft beer at Kapana or get lost in the Old Town's cobblestoned streets.
- If you want to spend one final day in nature, go to the Rhodope Mountains for bagpipe music, cliffside monasteries, and deep quiet.

💡 **Insider tips**

- **Many wineries:** allow walk-in samples, but for tours, phone or email ahead of time—you'll likely meet the winemaker.
- **Guesthouses over hotels**: In rural locations, pensiuni or family-run motels sometimes provide home-cooked meals and personal tales.

- **Pack layers:** since you'll be traveling through many climates, including mountains, plains, and vineyards.
- **Hire a car:** Especially in Maramureș and Melnik, where public transportation is limited.
- **Local festivities:** include wine harvest activities (September to October) and folk festivals in the summer.

This excursion brings together taste, mythology, and timeless landscape. You'll drink from hand-labeled bottles, learn folk dances in a barn, and walk away with mud on your boots and a happy heart.

6.3 Unusual Road Trip Ideas

The finest experiences don't always take a predictable path; instead, they follow your curiosity. If you're the kind of tourist who enjoys dead ends that lead to sheep pastures or wayside shrines that no guidebook mentions, these unique road excursions will be your favorite part of the vacation.

Route 1: Villages and Volcanoes (Hungary & Romania).

Debrecen to Hajdúszoboszló, then Oradea to Rimetea, and finally Turda.

- Visit Hajdúszoboszló, also known as Hungary's beach, to enjoy thermal baths.
- Cross into Romania and explore Art Nouveau Oradea, which is freshly polished and postcard-worthy.
- Sleep in Rimetea, a whitewashed town nestled among the breathtaking Piatra Secuiului cliffs.
- End at Turda Salt Mine, an underground amusement park made of salt.

Route 2: Forest Roads and Folklore (Romania, Bulgaria)

Route: Iași via Vrancea wine area, then Ruse to Veliko Tarnovo, and finally Shipka Pass.

- Begin in Iași, Romania's cultural capital.
- Sample sparkling wines at Odobești and Cotești before crossing the Danube in Ruse.
- Explore Veliko Tarnovo's castle remains, which overlook a spectacular canyon.

- Drive via Shipka Pass, one of Bulgaria's most picturesque mountain highways, featuring war monuments and panoramic vistas.

🚐 Route 3: Black Sea Byways, Bulgaria

Varna to Balchik, then to Kaliakra Cape, Tyulenovo, and finally Sozopol.

- Begin with sun and seafood in Varna.
- Stop at Balchik, where a Romanian queen constructed a coastal mansion and botanical garden.
- Explore the sea-carved rocks of Kaliakra and eat mussels at a cliffside farm in Tyulenovo.
- Relax in Sozopol, where artists, fishermen, and moonlight music meet together.

📍 Road trip reminders.

- 🚗 Renting a vehicle is reasonable, but make sure you have cross-border authorization.
- ⊛ Fuel outlets may be far apart in rural areas—fill up before mountain drives.
- Offline maps (e.g., Maps.me or Google Offline) are your best friend. Road signage differs greatly.

- ◼ Unplanned wayside shrines, stork nests, and granny-selling plums from a bucket add to the charm of the journey.
- ♥ Go slowly. Ask questions. Respond by waving back. This area rewards patience with experiences that do not fit into itineraries.

This is your license to travel slowly, carefully, and with wonder—to be "lost" on purpose and discover the tales that don't make the headlines but stick with you long after the journey home.

Chapter 7: Culture and Heritage.

Exploring the Soul of Central and Eastern Europe.

7.1 Shared histories and divergent paths

Traveling across Hungary, Romania, and Bulgaria, you begin to realize something: you can cross a border, but history cannot. One town may contain onion-domed churches with Cyrillic lettering, the next cobblestone courtyards with Baroque facades, and the third a calm Communist-era apartment building towering tall behind a 13th-century tower. It's not perplexing; it's the stunning intricacy of an area that has never ceased changing.

A landscape shaped by empires

For ages, these areas have been on the brink of empire—but never on the margins of civilization.

- **Hungary** was the center of the Austro-Hungarian Empire. That impact may still be seen in the Neo-Gothic parliament, stately coffeehouses, and the orderly elegance of towns like Budapest, Pécs, and Debrecen.

- **Romania**, despite its geographical location between East and West, retained a Latin language and cultural core while being influenced by Hungarian, Ottoman, Russian, and Austrian forces. Transylvania, in particular, seems like a mix of styles: Saxon villages, Hungarian strongholds, and Romanian Orthodox monasteries coexist.

- **Bulgaria,** governed by the Ottomans for almost five centuries, has a distinct visual memory. Mosques becoming museums, monasteries tucked away in woods, and Thracian graves cut into hills—all silently reveal tales of perseverance and survival.

Even recent history left its imprint. The Communist era, which is still vivid in memory, created enormous buildings, towering sculptures, and a common culture of stoicism and sarcasm. Former propaganda paintings have been redone as street art, abandoned party offices have been converted into startups, and Soviet-era industries now host techno parties and modern galleries.

How to Live This History Firsthand

1. 🏛 Visit Budapest's Memento Park, which houses historic Communist sculptures and serves as an open-air museum of ideology.
2. 🏰 Explore Saxon-walled villages in Sighisoara or Sibiu (Romania), including pastel houses and watchtowers built by German immigrants during the Middle Ages.
3. In Plovdiv, see the Dzhumaya Mosque, which is still functioning and located between a Roman stadium, Orthodox church, and Communist-era mural.
4. 🧍 Join a city walking tour guided by residents to hear frank family tales that make history seem real, personal, and immediate.

The history here is not limited to museums. It's in the café where revolutionaries once planned, the church bell cast in Ottoman silver, and the fading slogans still engraved on school walls. It's living, complicated, and sometimes delivered in whispers—but once you learn to listen, it never stops speaking.

7.2 Faith, Pilgrimage, and Sacred Sites

Religion in this area is more than simply religion; it is about belonging. Even in the most secular places, religious sites serve as anchors, uniting generations through ritual, architecture, and memory. Faith is softly woven into everyday life here, whether in the form of a cross carved into a mountain, a bright synagogue courtyard, or a procession of icons carried through local streets.

Orthodox Christianity: Icons, Incense, and Intimacy

Orthodox churches in Romania and Bulgaria are more than just places of worship; they represent centuries of spiritual activity.

- Stepping inside any monastery—Rila, Bachkovo, Horezu—you'll be surrounded by the aroma of beeswax, the brilliance of gold leaf, and the sound of mumbled prayers. Unlike Western churches, Orthodox interiors are warm, cozy, and rich in symbolism.
- Services are lengthy, primarily sung, and often require standing, however, guests are welcome as long as they are courteous. Cover your shoulders, avoid photos during worship, and take time to light

a candle or draw an icon—even if you're not devout, the ambiance is very affecting.

Wooden Churches in Romania: Humble and Holy

Maramureș and Bucovina include some of Europe's most beautiful—and often overlooked—religious buildings.

1. Many of these UNESCO-listed wooden churches are centuries old, constructed without nails, and have steeples that soar like fingers into the sky.
2. Inside, you'll see folk-painted paintings, low ceilings, and the lingering aroma of pinewood from decades.
3. On feast days, locals may welcome you with a basket of eggs or apples; hospitality and religion are inextricably linked here.

Jewish, Muslim, and Catholic Threads

Despite their tiny size today, Jewish and Muslim populations have had a long-term impact on the region's culture.

- Visit Budapest's Dohány Street Synagogue, Europe's biggest, and learn about the once-thriving Jewish enclave, which has a vibrant culinary and creative scene.

- Ottoman mosques may still be seen in Plovdiv and Sofia, with aged yet majestic minarets flanked by modest tea shops and kebab stalls.
- In Transylvania, Catholic history is preserved via Baroque churches and religious festivals, particularly in Hungarian-majority places like Csíksomlyó, where thousands come for yearly pilgrimages.

Pilgrimage is not only for the pious.

You do not need to be religious to go on a pilgrimage. In this region of Europe, religious locations are often located in lovely, calm settings that are suitable for introspection.

- Hike to St. Ivan's Cave near Rila Monastery. It combines a spiritual experience with a natural stroll.
- ■ Attend a major Orthodox event, such as Easter or Assumption Day, to celebrate religion via drumming, chanting, and community feasts.
- 🧎 Many monasteries offer retreats or overnight stays where you may read, write, or just sit quietly beneath historic murals.

Faith here is about continuity more than a formality, with rites handed down quietly in kitchens, wayside shrines, and hamlet bells that still mark the hours. Even if you merely come to watch, the serenity and genuineness of it all may leave you feeling moved.

7.3 Myths, Legends, and Superstitions.

Talk to enough natives in these nations and you'll notice something: folklore is alive. It's not hidden in children's literature; it's in lullabies, rituals, seasonal dances, and those strange tiny charms you see hanging on doorways or tree branches. These are more than simply tales; they represent the cultural undercurrent, combining pagan foundations with Christian ideas and centuries of creativity.

The Realm of Vampires, Forest Spirits, and Talking Wolves

- In Romania, vampires are more than simply tourist attractions. While Bram Stoker's Dracula is a work of fiction, the image of the strigoi—a restless spirit that emerges from the dead—is deeply embedded in local folklore, particularly in rural places. People still lay garlic on windowsills, bury the dead with cash, and burn the deceased's clothing to keep off unrestful spirits.
- Bulgarian folklore has samodivi, woodland fairies that dance in the moonlight and steal men's voices. Children are taught not to whistle after midnight lest they attract ghosts.

- Legends in Hungary include táltos (spirit healers) and Turul, a mythological bird thought to lead Hungarian fate, which is depicted on bridges and monuments around the nation.

Seasonal Rituals You May See (Or Join)

1. Mărțișor (March 1st) - In Romania and Bulgaria, people exchange red-and-white string bracelets as symbols of regeneration and brotherhood. Hang them on flowering trees to bring good luck.
2. Kukeri (January-February): In Bulgaria, men dress in extravagant fur and mask costumes with cowbells and conduct traditional dances to ward off bad spirits. Loud, cheerful, and mesmerizing.
3. Easter Witch Burning (Hungary): A spring tradition in which metaphorical witches (often straw dolls) are burnt in bonfires to ward off cold and disease.

Folk Magic and Everyday Superstitions

1. Don't whistle inside; it brings ill luck.
2. Never sit in the corner of a table; you will not marry.
3. Are you spilling salt? Throw it over your left shoulder.
4. Babies often wear red thread to fend off the evil eye.

These may seem to be outdated, yet locals do not dismiss them outright. They are regarded with a combination of respect, humor, and affection—rituals that, even in today's society, connect families and generations.

📍 Experience these traditions firsthand.

- Visit an ethnographic museum, such as those in Plovdiv, Sibiu, or Szentendre, to see traditional costumes, musical instruments, and everyday objects.
- Attend a local festival and inquire around, particularly in the spring and summer. Many are unpublicized yet quite significant.
- Look for homemade items like embroidered blouses, woodcarvings, and Martenitsa charms. They're more than simply keepsakes; they're storytellers.

Folklore here isn't kept in glass cases. It exists in ballads handed down over soup, in the whisper of trees at sunset, and in the way a grandma crosses herself as a storm approaches. It isn't about faith; it's about belonging to something older than language.

Chapter 8: Nature and Adventure.

Wilderness, Wellness, and The Call of the Wild

Some mornings begin with bells and lively city squares. Others begin gently, with dewdrops clinging to grass, boots crunching softly on woodland pathways, and a cloud of mist rising from a lake unconcerned about being photographed.

Hungary, Romania, and Bulgaria may not appear to be "adventure destinations" at first glance, but those who venture into their wild hearts discover a different kind of thrill—one shaped by untouched national parks, glacial lakes, howling wolves, hot springs, and sky-high passes once trodden by shepherds and saints.

If you're looking for a nature-filled retreat, whether it's relaxing in mineral-rich hot baths, trekking through alpine valleys, spelunking through extensive cave systems, or cycling amid vineyards, this is the place to go.

8.1 National Parks and Nature Reserves

This area features some of Europe's most biodiverse and least-explored natural environments. With protected areas extending from the Carpathian Mountains to the Danube Delta, it's a paradise for animal enthusiasts, bird watchers, hikers, and tranquility seekers alike.

Hungary: Gentle Hills and Wetland Wonders.

Hungary's environment may not be as striking as its neighbors, but it provides unexpected natural diversity and mellow, soul-soothing beauty.

- **Hortobágy National Park:** is Europe's biggest continuous natural grassland. You'll witness herds of native Hungarian grey cattle, cranes dancing in shallow rivers, and csikós (cowboys) executing incredible horse acrobatics.
- **Aggtelek National Park:** is a UNESCO World Heritage site known for the Baradla Cave system, which links to Slovakia beneath. Above the earth, there are several undulating hills, woodland pathways, and limestone cliffs.
- **Bükk National Park:** is Hungary's most wooded area, with oak and beech woods, wild orchids in

spring, and hidden waterfalls. Suitable for hikers and amateur botanists.

Insider tip: *Hungarian parks often contain information boards in Hungarian alone. Bring a translation app or take a guided tour to get the entire story.*

Romania: The Wild Carpathians

Nature lovers come here to disconnect from the outside world and reconnect with themselves. Romania's national parks are enormous, undeveloped, and very diversified.

- **Piatra Craiului National**: Park is known for its knife-edge limestone ridge, untamed meadows, and occasional sightings of chamois and brown bears. Rustic guesthouses in Zărneşti and Măgura provide excellent trail access.

- **Retezat National Park:** has glacial lakes, towering peaks, and some of Europe's purest air. Ideal for multi-day trips that include overnight stays in simple mountain huts (refuges) or tents.

- **Danube Delta Biosphere Reserve:** A wetland wonderland where the Danube River flows into the Black Sea. Over 300 bird species call this place home, as do otters, wild horses, and floating communities.

The best way to explore is via canoe, kayak, or slow boat with a local guide.

Wildlife Note: *Romania contains one of Europe's greatest populations of brown bears, wolves, and lynx. While sightings are uncommon, please follow local animal safety advice and stay on defined pathways.*

Bulgaria: Peaks, Pines, and Alpine Serenity.

Bulgaria's mountains are lyrical, panoramic, and full of possibilities, ranging from pristine alpine routes to verdant valleys filled with goat bells.

- **Rila National Park:** is home to the highest point in the Balkans, Musala Peak. The trails go past glacier lakes, wild blueberries, and the famed Seven Rila Lakes. Access via Borovets or Sapareva Banya.
- **Pirin National Park:** is a UNESCO site featuring steep terrain, marble peaks, and old pine woods. Base yourself at Bansko for convenient access and comfortable post-hike meals.
- **The Central Balkan National:** Park is known for its waterfalls, wild flora, and Bulgaria's famed Balkan flowers. Botev Peak and the Heavenly Path (Ray Trail) to the Ray Waterfall are must-see destinations.

- **Local Secret:** Look for herbal tea brewed from foraged mountain herbs; locals swear by its therapeutic properties and spiritual advantages.

There's more than just paths and trees wherever you go. You'll come across shepherds, monks, and mushroom gatherers. You'll sip crystal-clear mountain spring water that will astound your city senses. You will discover quiet that hums louder than city noise ever could.

8.2 Thermal Baths, Caves, and Natural Wonders.

Beyond the hills and woods, this area is home to natural wonders created by fire, water, and time. These are the spots that leave you wide-eyed and delightfully still as you float, descend, or stroll into another universe.

Soak and Soothe: Thermal Baths and Mineral Springs.

Hungary is the indisputable champion of thermal bathing. With more than 1,300 natural springs, it's a daily habit.

1. **Széchenyi Baths (Budapest)** are grand, outdoor, and renowned. Locals play chess in hot water as steam rises into the chilly air.

2. **Miskolctapolca Cave Bath:** A spa located inside a natural cave system, offering therapeutic waters in candlelit grottos.

3. **Hévíz Lake:**is the biggest ecologically active thermal lake in the world. Float in lily-covered waters warmed from below, even in December.

Romania and Bulgaria have their therapeutic hideaways.

- **Băile Herculane (Romania):** A historic Roman spa town nestled between cliffs and woodland. Austro-Hungarian baths have been restored, as have natural rock pools in the neighboring river.

- **Sapareva Banya (Bulgaria)** is home to Europe's hottest geyser. Excellent base for trekking Rila, followed by a lengthy bath.
- **Velingrad (Bulgaria)** is known as the Spa Capital of the Balkans. Imagine sophisticated health hotels, pine-scented air, and healing spring water.

Down to Earth: Caves and Subterranean Beauty.

The caves in this area are more than simply holes in the earth. They are subterranean cathedrals, sculpted over millennia into miracles of light, stone, and quiet.

- **Baradla Cave (Hungary):** Part of the Aggtelek-Karst system, this cave spans 26 kilometers, parts of which extend into Slovakia. Join a lantern-lit tour for a fairytale experience.
- **Scărişoara Ice Cave (Romania):** Even in the summer, you may go inside a glacier. A wooden staircase descends into frigid quiet and crystal-blue rooms.
- **Devetashka Cave (Bulgaria)** is enormous and open-roofed, with swallows flying across the light beams. You may remember it from action flicks, but it is most effective when perfectly motionless.

Color and Wonder: Unique Natural Formations.

1. **The Red Lake (Lacul Roșu)** in Romania is a natural dam lake with drowned pine trunks set against blood-red dirt cliffs.

2. **Belogradchik Rocks (Bulgaria)** are towering sandstone formations styled like animals and giants, with a medieval fortification constructed within them.

3. **The Stone Forest (Hungary):** Kővágóörs has strange volcanic structures rising from the fields, ideal for low-key exploring.

These natural treasures give more than just beauty. They return you to your senses, geologic time, and the profound silence that comes with being in a place older than human memory.

8.3 Adventure Activities

This area attracts not just tranquil nature lovers, but also adrenaline seekers, outdoor addicts, and those who want to earn their views with sweat and fun.

Hiking and Trekking

- **The Transfăgărăşan Highway (Romania)** is sometimes referred to as Europe's most gorgeous road, but the trails leading off it are even more spectacular. Climb to Bâlea Lake, then climb over ridgelines for panoramic views of the Carpathians.
- **The seven Rila Lakes in Bulgaria** are named after mythical features such as tears, eyes, kidneys, and so on. The circular trek may be completed in one day but will leave you with memories for a lifetime.
- **Zemplén Mountains (Hungary):** Forested, low-elevation, ideal for fall treks, birding, and castle hopping.

Cycling, Mountain Biking, and Vineyard Cruising

- **Tokaj Wine Region (Hungary):** Cycle through vineyards, apricot orchards, and peaceful churches, stopping for samples along the route.
- **Saxon Villages (Romania):** Rent bikes in Viscri, Biertan, or Criţ and ride over unpaved back roads lined with haystacks and painted gates.
- **Rhodope Mountains (Bulgaria):** A hidden treasure for mountain biking, with off-road tracks,

tough terrain, and some of the greatest handmade meals available at the end of the day.

Winter sports

- **Bansko and Borovets (Bulgaria):** Consistent snow, contemporary lifts, and a fraction of the cost of the Alps. Perfect for skiers and snowboarders of all skill levels.
- **Poiană Brașov (Romania):** A popular resort set in the Carpathians. Stay in Brașov for culture, ski during the day, and warm yourself with mulled wine at night.

- **Mátraszentistván (Hungary):** Sms.
- **Kayaking in the Danube Delta (Romania):** A languid, dreamy paddle among reeds, pealler and more easygoing, perfect for families and novices.

Water Adventures

- In the spring, whitewater rafting on the Jiu or Buzău Rivers (Romania) or the Struma River (Bulgaria) is fast-flowing, wild, and directed by expert guidelicans, and mirror-like water.
- For a relaxing summer experience, try stand-up paddleboarding (SUP) on Lake Balaton in Hungary or the Black Sea beaches in Bulgaria.

Whether you're looking for excitement or calm, the landscape of this area provides both wild freedom and grounded quiet, all without the crowds or expensive prices of Western Europe. In between each experience, there's always a warm supper, a friendly face, and a drink of something local to greet you home.

Chapter 9: Practical Travel Essentials.

Comfort, Confidence, and Common Sense for a Smooth Journey.

9.1 Accommodation Options

Arriving in a new place is exhilarating, but knowing where and how you will sleep may be the difference between travel stress and travel happiness. In Hungary, Romania, and Bulgaria, your lodging options are more than simply a place to sleep; they are part of the cultural experience, providing a deeper connection to the countries you visit.

🏛 Boutique Hotels and Mid-Range Comfort.

These are ideal if you value style and substance—places with smart design, excellent service, and a genuine local atmosphere without going overboard.

- In Budapest, boutique hotels often combine Art Nouveau charm with clean contemporary lines. Consider copper lighting, thermal-inspired treatment rooms, and rooftop drinking patios.
- In Plovdiv and Brașov, you may discover reconstructed 19th-century buildings with exposed

beams, vibrant paintings, and handcrafted local fabrics.

- Prices normally vary between €50 and €100 per night—a perfect spot for comfort, convenience, and value.

Insider Tip: Look for hotels branded "family-run" or "heritage"—they generally provide a prepared breakfast, insider city recommendations, and a level of friendliness that multinationals lack.

🐦 Guesthouses and Rural Retreats (Pensiune, Casa, and Selo Houses).

A country guesthouse is the ideal place for a slower, more soulful stay. Whether you wake up to roosters crowing in Maramureş or vine-covered patios in southern Bulgaria, these stays immerse you in the rhythms of local life.

- Romania's pensiune provides accommodations in family homes, with three-course meals prepared from their gardens.
- Clay ovens, pickled vegetables, and a grandfather reciting tales in the background are common features of Bulgarian selo households.

- Expect to spend between €20 and €60 each night, which includes substantial handmade meals and unlimited mountain tea.

Action Tip: *Always clarify that meals are included, inquire about heating in the winter and air conditioning in the summer, and carry cash—many remote accommodations do not accept credit cards.*

Hostels, City Apartments, and Budget Picks

1. Backpackers, lone travelers, and digital nomads rejoice—this area offers affordable travel without compromising charm.
2. Hostels in Sofia, Budapest, and Bucharest often include industrial-chic common areas, complimentary walking tours, and local beer on tap.
3. In smaller towns, you'll find comfortable dormitories, private rooms with communal kitchens, and friendly owners who will mark trails on your map.
4. Short-term rentals (such as Airbnb or Booking flats) are popular and beneficial for extended visits or individuals who like cooking their meals.

Watch out for reviews that highlight noise levels, true cleanliness, and heating in the cold. Also, if you're working remotely, make sure your Wi-Fi is reliable.

In these three nations, your lodging may become a chapter of your journey—a breakfast table turned language conversation, a balcony turned stargazing site, or a vintage sofa converted into a travel-planning headquarters for the following day's trip. Take the time to choose a stay that suits your speed and personality; it will be worthwhile.

9.2 Packing by Season.

This area has four distinct seasons, and packing correctly might be the difference between being invigorated to explore and facing the elements unprepared. The weather isn't dramatic, but it changes quickly—mountains are frigid, cities may be scorching, and spring showers strike without notice. **Let us break it down.**

❄ Winter (December–February)

Consider charming Christmas markets, snow-covered towns, and hot spas beneath a starry sky.

- 🧥 Bring a decent winter coat (preferably water-resistant), gloves, hat, and scarf.

- 🥾 Waterproof footwear is a must—cities salt their roadways, but rural areas may turn slushy.
- 🧦 Thermal leggings and layer-able sweaters are ideal for lengthy train trips and monastery visits.
- 🌲 Want to go to a Christmas village market? Look up Sibiu or Budapest's Vörösmarty Square and pack your warmest socks.

🌸 Spring (March to May)

- Blossoms blossom, fields green up, and the trekking season starts.
- 🌦 Prepare for unexpected weather by wearing light layers and a rain jacket.
- 👟 Pack waterproof shoes or light boots for rural hikes.
- In cities, jeans, a cardigan, and a light jacket may transport you from art galleries to hilltop strongholds.
- 🌺 If you're sensitive to pollen, remember to bring sunglasses and allergy medicines since this season is full of flower magnificence.

☀ Summer (June–August)

- This is when the area shines—long days, outdoor festivities, and Black Sea beach getaways.
- 👗 Light, breathable materials, such as linen and cotton, are ideal for the hot climate in Bucharest and Sofia.
- 🎩 Bring a wide-brimmed hat and a refillable water bottle to stay cool on hot days.
- 🩳 Pack modest clothing (knee-length shorts or skirts) for religious locations.
- 🩴 Wear flip-flops or water shoes on thermal lakes or pebble beaches.

🍂 Autumn (September to November)

- The underappreciated golden season—cold enough for lengthy walks but mild enough for café patios.
- 🧥 Dress warmly in layers, boots, and a medium-weight jacket for cold mornings and warmer afternoons.
- 📷 Fall colors are magnificent in Plovdiv's Old Town, Lake Balaton, and Bran Castle.
- 🍁 Bring a reusable bag or small daypack for market shopping and unplanned wine excursions.

General must-haves (year-round)

1. Travel umbrella or packable raincoat
2. Plug adaptor (European plug Type C or F)
3. Travel-sized pharmaceutical kit (band-aids, pain relievers, motion sickness medications).
4. Scarf or shawl for cold churches, unexpected winds, or dressing up.
5. You'll be recording steps, so wear comfortable walking shoes!

Traveling here rewards you for being prepared. Dress in layers, follow local dress codes in villages and religious places, and save some luggage room for embroidered blouses, pottery dishes, or handcrafted wool slippers—you'll thank yourself later.

9.3 Health, Safety, and Insurance

It's easy to get engrossed in castles, gastronomy, and cobblestone streets—but being prepared for your health and safety guarantees that your experience is spectacular from beginning to end.

Healthcare and Medical Care

Healthcare in this region is economical, dependable, and easily accessible, particularly in metropolitan regions.

- **Pharmacies (Apoteka / Gyógyszertár / Farmacie)** are ubiquitous and often the first visit. Many staff members understand basic English and can assist with minor diseases, cold medications, and bug stings.

- For more critical conditions, governmental hospitals are free or low-cost, while private clinics often provide speedier care and have English-speaking personnel.

- **EU/UK nationals having an EHIC/GHIC** card are protected for emergencies in Hungary and Bulgaria (to a lesser degree, Romania). Always verify locally.

- **Non-EU passengers** should make sure their travel insurance covers medical care, repatriation, and delays. Carry both a digital and paper copy of your insurance.

Tip: *Some rural areas are distant from medical facilities. If you suffer from allergies, asthma, or other diseases, bring your medicines and a short translated notice in the local language.*

🧴 Vaccines and Health Preparation

- There are no particular vaccines necessary for entrance.
- If you want to go on country treks, explore caves, or deal with animals, you should have your tetanus, hepatitis A, and rabies shots updated.
- Tap water is safe to drink in cities across Hungary and Bulgaria. In Romania, consult locals—it varies by area.
- Mosquitoes and ticks are frequent in marshes and meadows, so bring insect repellent for your summer forest treks.

👤 Safety and Common Sense.

- These nations are very secure for tourists, particularly single and female visitors. However, as usual, be watchful and streetwise.
- Pickpocketing may occur on crowded public transportation (particularly the Budapest and Sofia metros), therefore carry a money belt or crossbody purse.
- Avoid unlicensed cabs and instead use Bolt or trustworthy apps, particularly late at night.

- Watch for currency exchange scams around train stations—always use banks or licensed exchange counters.

Emergency Numbers (Works Across the EU/EEA):

1. 🔔 112: General Emergency (police, ambulance, fire)
2. 🩺 Bring a list of allergies, medicines, blood type, and a local contact (if applicable).

🧠 Final Essentials

1. Create digital backups of your passport, health cards, tickets, and insurance.
2. Have a modest first-aid kit with pain relievers, plasters, anti-diarrhea, allergy medications, and antiseptic cream.
3. Keep a few keywords written down or stored in translation software, particularly if traveling alone in rural regions.

Being prepared does not imply being paranoid. It means traveling with confidence, knowing you're covered—whether you bump your toe on cobblestones, require allergy medication in a mountain hamlet, or just want comfort that you can deal with a surprising delay calmly.

9.4 Staying Connected

Whether you're tweeting your first glimpse of the Danube, navigating to a secret monastery, or phoning your guesthouse to let them know you're running late, being connected when traveling isn't a luxury—it's a must. Fortunately, staying online is simple, inexpensive, and convenient for travelers in Hungary, Romania, and Bulgaria.

▌ Should you get a local SIM card?

Yes, if you want to remain for more than a few days or go off the tourist track.

1. A local SIM card provides you with inexpensive Internet, clear calls, and the ability to easily book cabs, check train timetables, translate menus, and WhatsApp your host.

2. Prepaid plans are readily available, starting at €5-10 and providing ample data for navigation, streaming, and video chats.

All three nations are in the EU roaming zone, so if you buy a SIM in one of them, it should function across borders without additional charges—but double-check this before purchasing.

📡 Top SIM providers by country.

🇭🇺 Hungary

- Yettel (previously Telenor), Vodafone, and Magyar Telekom are the leading contenders.
- Look for prepaid tourist plans (for example, Yettel offers 10GB+ bundles).
- Available at airports, shopping malls, phone shops, and even certain post offices.

🇷🇴 Romania

- Orange, Vodafone, and Digi (RCS/RDS) dominate the market.
- Digi is relatively inexpensive, however, it provides significantly less coverage in distant regions.
- SIM cards are available in newsstands, petrol stations, and telecom stores; however, passport registration is necessary.

🇧🇬 Bulgaria

- A1, Vivacom, and Yettel are the leading suppliers.
- You can get 7-15GB for about €5-8, which includes calls and messages.
- Easy to purchase in airports, kiosks, and retail malls.

▮ Wi-Fi Access and Café Culture

- Free Wi-Fi is available everywhere—and it's fairly fast.

- Most hotels, hostels, cafés, restaurants, and rail stations have free Wi-Fi.
- Major cities, such as Budapest, Sofia, and Bucharest, provide public Wi-Fi zones throughout their tourist districts.
- Many remote guesthouses and mountain getaways also provide access; just ask for the password (which is commonly posted to the fridge or near reception).

Insider Tip: Wi-Fi in some distant communities may be sluggish or inconsistent, particularly in weather-sensitive mountain locations. If you're working remotely or need a good connection, read reviews or confirm with your host before booking.

✈ **At the airport? Here's how to go online quickly.**

- Vodafone and Yettel booths may be found in the arrivals area at Budapest Airport.
- Orange and Vodafone offer kiosks at Bucharest Henri Coandă Airport, and you can also get SIM packs at convenience shops.
- Sofia Airport: A1 and Vivacom offer vending machines and stands after security.

Tip: *Bring your unlocked phone. Most European SIM cards will not operate if your phone is locked to your home network. Whether you're booking trains on the go, sharing your Black Sea sunset, or just checking when the next event begins, being connected keeps you spontaneous and stress-free. And with affordable costs and excellent coverage, it's simpler than ever to travel smart while being sociable.*

9.5 Currency and Tip Culture

While many businesses now take credit cards, learning how to manage local money, avoid hidden costs, and tip like a local may make your vacation seem more seamless and respectful—as well as prevent those uncomfortable "is this enough?" moments at dinner or the taxi stand.

💲¥ Understanding Currency

- Hungary uses the Hungarian Forint (HUF). You'll notice notes for 1,000, 5,000, and 10,000 forints. €1 ≈ 385-400 HUF.

- Romania's official currency is the Romanian Leu (RON). Prices are often rounded. €1 ≈ 5 RON.

- Bulgaria uses the Bulgarian Lev (BGN). Pronounced "lev." €1 is about 1.95 BGN.

Where to Get Cash?

- ATMs are commonly accessible and provide the most favorable conversion rates.

- To avoid expensive fees and fraud, use legitimate bank ATMs (OTP, Unicredit, Banca Transilvania, Raiffeisen, or DSK).

- Turn down the ATM's conversion offer ("Do you want to convert to your home currency?") and let your bank handle it; you'll save money every time.

Avoid ATMs at airports and tourism shops. If it glows like a slot machine, it's usually a scam.

◼ Card or cash?

1. Cities: Visa and MasterCard are readily accepted. American Express is less prevalent.
2. Markets, taxis, remote guesthouses, and local buses sometimes need cash.
3. Bring some tiny dollars and coins, particularly for gratuities, snacks, bus tickets, and little souvenir stores.

✹ Tips Culture: A Quick Guide

Tipping is required but not exorbitant. Locals tip modestly and casually—you won't insult anybody by getting it a little incorrect, but here's what's regarded polite:

Restaurants

1. 10% is usual; more if the service is extraordinary.
2. Check to see whether a service fee is already included (search for "services" or "taxă de service").
3. In certain local restaurants, round up or leave a modest change instead of calculating percentages.

Cafés and Bars

1. Rounding up is ok.
2. Leave a few bucks or a tiny note if you lingered or had outstanding service.

Taxis

1. Although it is not needed, rounding up to the closest full number is much appreciated.
2. For example, if your journey costs 38 RON, paying 40 is quite acceptable.

Hotel staff

1. Porters charge €1–2 per bag.
2. Housekeeping fee: €1-2 each night, placed on the pillow or nightstand.
3. Tipping is uncommon, but always appreciated when they go out of their way.

Tour Guides

1. Group trips cost €5–10 per person.
2. Private guides or multi-day trips cost between €10 and €20 per day, depending on the duration and service.

⬤ Currency and Local Quirks

1. Some rural establishments may not have change for big sums, so have coins and small notes on hand.

2. Never accept cash from street exchangers, especially if they promise "better" rates. Stick to banks and ATMs.

3. If you're visiting all three countries, be sure to convert any remaining cash before crossing borders—it might be difficult to exchange HUF, RON, or BGN outside of their respective nations.

❖❖❖ Travel Smart Habits

1. When walking through crowded train stations or marketplaces, carry a tiny crossbody purse or money belt.

2. In case of loss, save a digitally encrypted picture of your card data and passport.

3. To save costs, carry a travel-friendly debit card such as Revolut, Wise, or N26 that does not impose foreign withdrawal or exchange fees.

With a little preparation, you'll be able to conquer the money game here in no time—spending wisely, tipping confidently, and always having enough to say yes to a last-minute food market or riverfront café.

Chapter 10: Cultural Immersion and Inspiration.

Stories, sounds, and souvenirs from the Balkans that will stay with you

Every traveler returns with photographs. But the items that stick with you—the ones that remain long after the luggage is unpacked—are the songs you heard floating through open windows, the words you read on the train trip between cities, and the surprise gifts that still smell like a village market.

Hungary, Romania, and Bulgaria are home to storytellers, artisans, folk singers, and filmmakers whose works capture the complex, soulful essence of the Balkans. If you're the kind of traveler who wants to bring your adventure home with you—not only in postcards but also in perspective—this chapter is for you.

10.1 Book, Film, and Music

Cultural understanding does not begin at the airport; rather, it may begin much earlier, with a book in your hands or music in your headphones. And it lasts long after you leave when a sentence from a movie or a folk song transports you back to a street café in Cluj or a smokey ruin bar in Budapest.

Here's a carefully chosen, thoroughly local collection to help you feel inspired, grounded, and connected.

🔹 Books to Read Before, During, and After Your Trip

Hungary

- **"Fatelessness"** by Imre Kertész is a sad, semi-autobiographical book about a Hungarian Jewish boy's experiences in Nazi death camps. It's thoughtful, quiet, and memorable.
- **"Budapest Noir"** by Vilmos Kondor combines gritty 1930s detective fiction with pre-war political turmoil. The excellent company on train travel to the capital.
- "T**he Door"** by Magda Szabó is a compelling female-centered book set in postwar Hungary that explores memory, identity, and societal change.

Romania

- **"The Land of Green Plums"** by Herta Müller is a terrifying portrayal of life under Ceaușescu's surveillance regime, presented in lyrical minimalism.

- **"Dracula"** by Bram Stoker is a British novel that introduced the world to Transylvania. When I read it again in Transylvania, it seems different.
- **"Balkan Ghosts"** by Robert D. Kaplan combines journalism, travel, and historical reflection to examine Eastern Europe's broken identities.

Bulgaria

- **"Under the Yoke"** by Ivan Vazov - A classic of Bulgarian literature on the April Uprising against Ottoman authority. Locals must complete their school reading.
- **"Street Without a Name"** by Kapka Kassabova is a book about growing up behind the Iron Curtain that is both nostalgic and insightful.
- **Kassabova's "Border"** is a travelogue and psychological investigation of the tri-border area of Bulgaria, Turkey, and Greece.

Films Bringing the Region to Life

Hungary

- **"Son of Saul"** is an Academy Award-winning, powerful Holocaust drama. The film is shot solely from the perspective of one individual, making it intense and demanding.

- **"Kontroll"** is a dark, surreal thriller set on the Budapest metro. Cult status for a good cause.
- **"On Body and Soul"** is a beautiful love tale about two lonely slaughterhouse workers who are bonded by their common aspirations. Eerie, peaceful, and gorgeous.

Romania

- **"4 Months, 3 Weeks, and 2 Days"** - the Palme d'Or-winning Romanian New Wave masterpiece. Gritty, riveting, set in communist-era Bucharest.
- **"The Death of Mr. Lazarescu"** combines dark humor with incisive social satire. You'll never look at a healthcare system the same again.
- **"Graduation"** - A father's silent yearning to provide a better future for his daughter exposes the undercurrents of corruption and moral compromise.

Bulgaria

- **"Glory"** - A train worker discovers a bag of money and turns it in before disappearing into a labyrinth of media spin and governmental machinery. Satirical, cutting, and devastating.
- **"The World** Is Big and Salvation Lurks Around the Corner" - A grandpa rides his grandson around

Europe on a tandem bicycle. Road movie meets soul seeking.

- **"Zift"** is a stylish black-and-white noir set in Sofia, combining communist-era brutality with Tarantino-esque flair.

Music that captures the essence of the Balkans.

Hungary

1. **Liszt and Bartók** - Begin with sweeping classical pieces with folk origins.
2. **Parno Graszt** - A Roma band whose music resembles a live street fair.
3. **Bohemian Betyars** is a Hungarian ska-punk with a touch of traditional flare.

Romania

1. **Fanfare Ciocărlia** - A fast-paced brass band from northeast Romania. Imagine trumpets, cymbals, and full-body dancing.
2. **Subcarpați** - A contemporary blend of hip-hop, folk, and protest.
3. **Maria Tănase** - Romania's Edith Piaf. Emotional and timeless.

Bulgaria

1. The **Mystery of the Bulgarian Voices** is an ethereal all-female choir whose haunting harmonies have gained worldwide acclaim.

2. **Valya Balkanska's** song "Izlel ye Delyo Haydutin" was carried into space on the Voyager Golden Record.

3. **Kottarashky** is a danceable combination of digital and traditional music. Think rhythms and bagpipes.

Whether you're reading a book on the train or creating a trip playlist, these tales and sounds let you tune into the emotional vibrations of the location, providing an opportunity to connect beyond mere sightseeing.

10.2 Souvenirs to Bring Home

Souvenirs should be mementos, not clichés. The greatest ones here are handcrafted, anchored in tradition, and exude the vitality of local artists who still work with love and patience.

H U Hungary

- **Kalocsa or Matyó embroidery** consists of vivid reds, blues, and greens worked onto linen and used for tablecloths, blouses, or wall art.
- **Paprika and spice sets** - Choose from sweet, spicy, or smoked variations in hand-painted jars or wooden tubes.
- **Porcelain** from Herend or Zsolnay is elegant, complex, and admired worldwide. Not inexpensive, but worth seeing at a museum.
- **Tokaji wine,** particularly the golden, sweet Aszú. Get a bottle with a date and drink it years later on a rainy day.

R O Romania

- **Painted Easter eggs (ouă încondeiate)** are often manufactured year-round and carefully painted with beeswax and dye. Symbolic and gorgeous.
- **Wooden carvings i**nclude spoons, icons, and spindle chairs, particularly from Maramureş.
- **Ie (traditional blouse)** - Each area has its theme. Authentic ones are hand-stitched and typically handed down through generations.

150

- **Plum brandy (ţuică)** - It will warm your bones while shocking your palette. Frequently manufactured and sold in repurposed soda bottles.

B G Bulgaria

- **Rose oil goods** from the Rose Valley include soaps, lotions, and little vials of concentrated rose oil with an ancient beauty history.
- **Troyan Pottery** has deep earth tones and whirling designs. Beautiful and useful.
- **Marteniţa** - Wear red and white threads from March 1 till you witness the first stork. Represents spring, rebirth, and local delight.
- **Wool crafts** include blankets, stockings, and slippers made of thick handwoven wool, which are ideal for cold winter days.

🍷 **Pro Tip:** *For the most genuine findings, visit local artisan markets, village festivals, or museum gift stores. Don't be afraid to question sellers about the origin of their products. Often, stories are included with the purchase.*

10.3 Responsible Travel Tips

Travel is more than simply going somewhere; it's also about how you get there. This natural and culturally rich area flourishes when tourists approach it as a shared home rather than a playground.

● Always support local businesses!

1. **Eat at family-owned eateries,** particularly in rural towns. Your supper may help send someone's child to university.
2. **Instead of commercial hotels,** stay in local guesthouses or family pensions; they will tell you tales as you eat your soup.
3. **Purchase straight** from craftsmen and merchants. Ask them where their art originates from, and you'll both grin more.

♻ Travel lightly on land.

Refill your water bottle; tap water is safe in most cities. Avoid single-use plastics.

Take your waste out of woods, parks, and trails; rural locations may not usually have enough cleaning facilities.

Use public transportation wherever feasible, or choose trains over short flights.

💛 Respect tradition and sacred spaces.

- When entering churches, synagogues, and monasteries, dress modestly by covering your shoulders and knees and removing your hat.
- Do not photograph anyone without their permission, particularly the elderly, market sellers, or those in prayer.
- Learn a d "Blagodarya" (BG)—a simple thank-you in the native tongue goes a long way.few phrases like "Köszönöm" (HU), "Mulţumesc" (RO), an

🙌 Be curious and not critical.

You may come into unexpected or challenging experiences, such as differing social standards, rural poverty, or graffiti expressing post-communist disenchantment.

Ask questions. Listen more than you talk. Growth occurs here as well.

When you choose to travel with awareness, openness, and cultural sensitivity, you become a member of a shared narrative rather than simply a guest. One where your influence and curiosity are important.

Chapter 11: Maps and Travel Tools.

Sometimes the most powerful aspect of travel is not having a flawless plan—it's just knowing where you are, how to go to the next location, and how to seek assistance if you get lost. Whether you're strolling through a historical city plaza or waiting on a mountain rail station in a rural community, the correct map, tool, or word may transform bewilderment into confidence.

This chapter is your go-to arsenal, packed with pictures, logistics, and linguistic necessities to help you travel across Hungary, Romania, and Bulgaria with purpose, peace of mind, and maybe even a little fun spontaneity.

11.1 Annotated Maps

When traversing a place with deep history, intricate terrain, and locally prized hidden jewels, no ordinary map will suffice. You want something that provides context, explains why something is important, and allows you to plan, explore, and dream a bit.

This book contains specially annotated maps to help you make sense of it all, complete with icons, color zones, and annotations that go well beyond those seen in regular travel programs.

What You'll Find on These Maps:

- Castles, fortifications, and medieval remains range from Vajdahunyad in Romania to the Rila Fortress Trails in Bulgaria.
- Hévíz and Miskolctapolca Cave Baths are among Hungary's popular thermal baths and wellness towns.
- UNESCO World Heritage Sites include Hollókő Village, Sighișoara Citadel, and the Boyana Church near Sofia.
- Scenic itineraries include wine tours, cycling around Lake Balaton, and driving the Transfagarasan Highway.
- Local culinary highlights include symbols for marketplaces, pastry hotspots, and notable wine-producing regions.

Each map is region-specific, therefore you'll discover different graphics for:

- **Hungary's Wine Trails and Thermal Circuits**
- **Romanian Castles, Saxon Villages, and Carpathian Routes**

- **Bulgaria's Mountains, Monasteries, and Coastal Treasures**

📌 How to use these maps.

- **Pre-trip planning:** Determine your must-sees and highlight cities or trails that match your speed.
- **On-the-ground guidance:** Use them for day excursions, particularly in remote areas with insufficient signage.
- **Offline trip backup:** Save digital copies to your phone and download them for offline access.

Insider Tip: Pair these maps with fliers from the local tourist office or museum maps—many small towns have hand-drawn or hyper-local maps that are not available online. They're both lovely and really practical.

11.2 Airports, Trains, and Transit Hubs.

Moving between cities and nations is part of the adventure—and, in many cases, a cultural experience. You'll hear a variety of languages, dialects, train announcements, and unexpected delays—but you'll also encounter some of the most friendly individuals at little stations, who'll gesture their way into directing you right.

Here's your go-to list of major transportation hubs, how to get around them, and the local logistics that will make you feel like a seasoned traveler, even if it's your first trip.

✈ Major airports (international and regional)

Hungary

- **Budapest Ferenc Liszt (BUD)** - A major hub. Efficient arrangement with English signs. Use the 100E airport express bus to reach the city center in around 35 minutes.
- **Debrecen (DEB)** - Smaller and more regional. Good for low-cost flights to eastern Hungary.

Romania

- **Bucharest Henri Coandă (OTP)** is Romania's busiest. To get to Gara de Nord (the major station), use the 780 or 783 bus routes or the recently enhanced rail service.
- **Cluj-Napoca (CLJ)** and Timişoara (TSR) provide convenient regional flights across the Balkans and Central Europe.

Bulgaria

- **Sofia (SOF)** - A well-organized, metro-connected airport with increasing international access.

- **Varna (VAR) and Burgas (BOJ)** serve coastal cities during the summer peak season. Frequently utilized by beachgoers and cruise ship passengers.

🚊 Train travel: scenic and cultural.

Train culture in this area is a rite of passage—it may not always be speedy, but it is always evocative.

Key hubs:

- **Keleti Station (Budapest)** has grand architecture and contemporary platforms. International lines to Vienna, Prague, and Belgrade.
- **Gara de Nord (Bucharest)** - Busy and functioning. Use applications such as CFR Calatori to monitor trains and purchase tickets.
- **Sofia Central Railway Station** was recently rebuilt. Connects with Plovdiv, Ruse, and Belgrade.

Pro Tip:

- Purchase tickets online or at official kiosks; avoid dodgy resellers near entrances.
- Trains may be sluggish yet picturesque, particularly the Bucharest to Brașov route through the Carpathians and Sofia to Veliko Tarnovo.

- Bring food, Kleenex, and offline entertainment, particularly for overnight trips.

🚌 Regional buses and minibuses (marshrutka).

Buses reign in locations where trains do not reach (or go at a sluggish pace).

1. FlixBus provides convenient intercity transportation with app-based booking.
2. Local mini buses (known as "marshrutka" in Bulgaria) are generally rapid, cash-only, and quirky—but inexpensive and efficient.
3. Intercity bus stations in Romania and Bulgaria may be somewhat hectic. Look for printed paper signs, and personnel at little booths, and don't be afraid to inquire.

🔵 Urban Transportation Tips

1. Budapest boasts a world-class metro system (including M1, the oldest continental subway line), trams, and buses. Purchase a 24/72-hour pass for unlimited travel.
2. Bucharest Metro is clean and fast, with multilingual signs but limited coverage.
3. Sofia's metro is modern, stylish, and connected to the airport—a rarity in the Balkans!

Don't forget that many rural communities and villages lack Uber and Bolt, and there are few public transportation choices. Coordinate transfers with your accommodation or plan ahead of time by researching regional bus timetables.

11.3. Quick Language Phrasebook

You don't have to be bilingual, but a few careful phrases may elevate your trip experience from tourist to really welcoming. People here admire the effort, and even poor pronunciation results in smiles, discounts, and more dishes. Here's a pocket-sized phrasebook full of useful, courteous, and uplifting phrases.

🐾 Polite Essentials

English	Hungarian (HU)	Romanian (RO)	Bulgarian (BG)
Hello	Helló / Szia	Bună / Salut	Zdrasti (Здрасти)
Thank you	Köszönöm	Mulțumesc	Blagodarya (Благодаря)

Please	Kérem	Vă rog	Molya (Моля)
Yes / No	Igen / Nem	Da / Nu	Da / Ne
Excuse me / Sorry	Bocsánat	Scuzaţi-mă / Îmi pare rău	Izvinete (Извинете)

🍴 Dining and Shopping

English	Hungarian	Romanian	Bulgarian
I'd like...	Szeretnék...	Aş dori...	Bikh iskam... (Бих искал...)
How much is it?	Mennyibe kerül?	Cât costă?	Kolko struva? (Колко струва?)
The bill, please	A számlát, kérem	Nota, vă rog	Smetkata, molya (Сметката, моля)

English	Hungarian	Romanian	Bulgarian
Delicious!	Finom!	Delicious!	Vkusno e! (Вкусно е!)
Water / Wine / Beer	Víz / Bor / Sör	Apă / Vin / Bere	Voda / Vino / Birra (Вода / Вино / Бира)

How to get around

English	Hungarian	Romanian	Bulgarian
Where is the station?	Hol van az állomás?	Unde este gara?	Kade e garata? (Къде е гарата?)
I need a taxi	Kellene egy taxi	Am nevoie de un taxi	Imam nuzhda ot taksi (Имам нужда от такси)
Do you speak English?	Beszél angolul?	Vorbiți engleză?	Govorite li angliyski? (Говорите ли английски?)

| Help! | Segítség! | Ajutor! | Pomoshch! |
| | | | (Помощ!) |

🗣 Tips on Speaking Up

1. Don't worry about the accent; locals appreciate the effort.

2. Download Google Translate with offline packs (particularly for Bulgarian Cyrillic).

3. Save screenshots of hotel names, maps, and locations in the local language for use when asking for directions.

Printed in Dunstable, United Kingdom